GLOBALISATION : AN ANTI-TEXT
A Local View

GLOBALISATION
AN ANTI-TEXT
A Local View

Pranab Kanti Basu

AAKAR

GLOBALISATION : AN ANTI-TEXT
A Local View
Pranab Kanti Basu

First Published, 2009

ISBN 978-81-89833-54-1 (Pb)

Published by
AAKAR BOOKS
28 E Pocket IV, Mayur Vihar Phase I, Delhi-110 091
Phone : 011-2279 5505 Telefax : 011-2279 5641
aakarbooks@gmail.com; www.aakarbooks.com

Printed at
Arpitprintographers, Shahdara, Delhi-110 032

To

the victims of development

Contents

Preface

Much of this book was written as a series of articles for a vernacular bimonthly with which I was associated. To understand the objective and scope of this book, it is helpful if the reader has some idea of the purpose behind both the bimonthly and the series of articles from which this book emerged. The bimonthly, *ekhon sanhathi,* which translates roughly into 'unity now', grew out of the need felt by a group of individuals, democratic organisations and trade unions to create a platform where diverse progressive views could be articulated both in the sense of expression as well as interaction. We all got together after the terrible Gujarat riots of 2002. It was a coming together of minds, which were united in their sorrow, shame and anger that these terrible acts of murder, rape, and pillage were perpetrated in the very country we called our own; that the state was a silent spectator, if not, as a lot of the media stories suggested, an active accomplice. We were also united in our faith in some kind of leftism, though we had differences regarding what leftism meant.

We all agreed on another point. The need at this critical juncture was to revive, refashion and spread a culture of some kind of left humanism, call it Marxism if you will. The need was for positive thought, not just condemnation.

A numbing culture of self-aggrandisement had permeated all the capillaries of social and personal being. This was sustaining and being sustained by various kinds of fanatical groupings. You cut all your community moorings. You are left to face economic, social and private crises all on your own. It gets too much. You leave reality behind, take to drugs, commit suicide. Or you fall into the waiting arms of fanatics who image your community for you. You define yourself by your new community alone. This is bound to be a definition in difference. So you learn to attribute all your miseries to the others – the other community. From there to fanaticism, to fanatical violence. It was simply insufficient to condemn this culture of individualism– which the mainstream economists applaud as 'rational'. One had to positively think of a new culture. The task was one of constructing a new ethos, a new community. We are not suggesting that one relegate to oblivion, the task of working towards a future in which those who toiled would no longer be servants. But this too was contingent on the birth of a new being for humankind. One could not just leave it to a master plan conceived by the PARTY. Surely the denouement of this simple project was there for all to see. So, while one had to struggle against the tyranny of the existing order, against the order itself, one had also to define the dream of the future, to construct the future in the mind. And since we all believe in materialism, this ethico-political task was inseparably linked to material construction. Thus to the practice of 'construction and struggle' – a particularly imaginative application of materialism, which had been articulated by one of the unsung heroes of peoples' movements in India, Shankar Guha Neogi.[1]

We thought of various ways in which we could contribute a tiny bit to this project. One of the ideas that emerged was the publication of a paper, which would be a kind of news magazine that would weigh current events and movements from a critical outlook. Unlike similar ventures, which were generally run by some monolithic organisation, which was either a party or verging on it, ours would be a democratic forum with the express purpose of exciting the mind of the reader to be critical. In plain terms, we would not judge a written piece by the known political antecedents of the writer. As long as we found the view coherent and broadly left in inclination, it would be acceptable.

Further, we would actively try to gather together conflicting opinions (or perspectives) on issues that we deemed to be important.[2] We felt that, apart from serving up news about current events from a critical perspective, we had to make people think about the chronic sores that our 'progress' was inflicting on our material and psychic being. At the same time, we had to be positive, bringing to light people's efforts, however small, to seek an alternative course of development.

One of the 'long-term' issues that had to be seriously analysed was globalisation. Generally, one can categorise the writings on such issues from a left perspective into three compartments: there are the erudite or elite pieces, full of impenetrable jargon, meant for the initiated; the pieces meant for plebeian readers where the writer gives tantalising glimpses of one's own knowledge of the theoretical issues involved but does not explicate the issues for the 'ignorant' reader; and then there are the pieces commissioned by the Party, whichever it may be. We felt that if the issue was one of building critical awareness, one could not shy away from introducing the reader to theoretical issues. At the same time, it was necessary to avoid obfuscating jargon.

So emerged the series of articles that was ultimately to take the shape of this present volume. While the series was appearing in Bengali, some of us felt that if the event that had immediately roused us from our complacent everyday slumber had occurred outside our state, there was reason to break out of our insularity and communicate with people outside our state. The best option was to articulate our position in Hindi. But that was ruled out by my linguistic limitations! Ultimately, we decided that it would be appropriate to write the book in English. By then the limitations of a democratic organisation had begun to surface and by the time I had completed the work of writing, the organisation had dissolved. However, I must acknowledge my debt to all those who were part of the organisation for motivating my effort.

Beyond this circle I am indebted to a lot of friends in Kolkata, especially those associated with the Economics Department of Calcutta University, who are actively baking new building blocks for political economy. Their work has helped in the formation/articulation of my ideas even where I disagree with their formulations. I have acknowledged my particular debts to them in the appropriate places.

Some I have to mention separately because they have contributed in ways that cannot be pinned down to some particular ideas or concepts. Ajit Chowdhury has been a philosopher and guide to me. Unfortunately, physical distance has prevented a more active collaboration in this particular project. Dipankar Das is an incisive, heartless critique and imaginative support in all my recent academic ventures. I am also grateful to him for doing a great job of editing most of the chapters. Rajesh Bhattacharya has also been an active participant for some of the journey.

I am always grateful to my daughter, Sreeja, for her unflagging desire to see my work in print. That is a great impetus. Finally, I am grateful to my wife, Nilanjana, for her sustained cynicism about our tendency towards intellectualism. This has spurred continuous self-criticism about the general readability and relevance of the views expressed.

Santiniketan, 2008 Pranab Kanti Basu

NOTES

1. Neogi is a neglected figure in the Indian Marxist pantheon. His innovative contributions both to the theory and practice of Marxism are discussed in some detail in Chapter 8.
2. Democracy is so much easier demanded than practised! Thousands of groups, like ours, have claimed to be different, that is, more democratic than others. How do you run a news magazine democratically? After all, you must have an editor. The problem is always essentially the same – can you have an organisation that is thoroughly democratic? Is there not a contradiction in terms? All that we can claim in our favour is that we were conscious of these issues. And, perhaps the best proof of our democratic credentials is that the group simply disintegrated when faced with internal disagreement over perspectives to a contemporary struggle! It did not preserve itself by expelling the minority. But then this is hardly a practicable solution to the dilemma.

1

Introduction

In this book I have attempted to present my ideas in a way that does not require any prior exposure of the reader to the theoretical approaches on which these ideas are constructed. Neither is a prior knowledge of economics – which is the stuff of globalisation – demanded. But, we believe that to form an educated opinion about the functioning of the global economy today, a minimum awareness of certain economic theoretic and accounting ideas is necessary. One has to know, for example, what a deficit in the balance of trade is; or what devaluation is supposed to achieve. Frequently, because of the lack of awareness of such issues, opponents of 'globalisation' today attribute all its ills to some naïve conspiracy theory. Where we have thought it necessary, we have introduced the readers to some theoretical issues. For example, we have elaborated upon such issues as mechanism of international trade, the neoclassical arguments for devaluation, etc. These have been done in a way that does not require any previous grounding in the discipline. So, in some sense *one can also use this as the common person's guide to the logic of international economic organisations in the age of globalisation*, though written from a particular perspective, but then, which tract is not? Because the book argues against the ruling orthodox opinion about the nature and benefits of globalisation, I have called it an *anti-text of globalisation*. A primary focus of the book is the debunking of the orthodox or neoclassical economic theoretic ideas that function as the underlying theoretical support in the defence of globalisation. We have tried to do this in a way that should not jar on the ears of those uninitiated to the discipline of economics. After all, they form the larger segment of the intended readership.

At the same time I have not consciously shied away from using those recent turns in the writing of political economy, which I believe would lead us to a land of some promise. I am mentioning those in this introduction and will revisit the issue in the concluding chapter. This is more in the way of situating our point of view and it is not mandatory on the part of the reader to navigate through these rarefied spaces in order to appreciate our understanding of globalisation. The rest of this introduction and the concluding chapter try to bring into focus the theoretical approach that we have adopted in our analysis. These parts may be skipped by readers who go through the book with the intention of simply getting a different view of what globalisation is all about. But those who believe that they are in some way committed to organising counter-hegemonic practice should go through them. As we discuss in a later chapter, one of the serious impediments to the development of counter-hegemonic practice has been the (structurally generated) unwillingness of major organised leftist movements to engage in polemics and the attendant aversion to equip their rank and file theoretically. So, in spite of the density of these segments, compared to the rest of the book, the latter group of readers should read these segments.

Our approach is based on a supplement to the notion of overdetermination, which was developed by the Althusserian or post-modern school of Marxism.[1] The particular supplement, which has influenced us most, is that developed in the seminal work, *margin of margin*.[2] Our purpose is to develop a possible theoretical approach to the phenomenon called globalisation. In spite of all the sound and fury about the need for leaving everything to the market, so-called liberalisation (or doing away with restrictions on free commerce) is but a small part of the current requirement of the capital that dominates the global scene. What is deliberately excluded from all the debates is the need for creation of the conditions for expansion of the market

– a process which, we claim, is an extension of *primitive capital accumulation*. This is simultaneously a process of dispossession of the traditional community rights as well as one of strengthening the power of global capital to extract rent. By occupation of territories and by creating or strengthening barriers to mobility of resources, global capital can extract rent[3] from bounded spaces. We argue that globalisation involves fundamentally the process of annulment of community rights and even individual bourgeois legal rights (where they conflict with the drive by global capital to extract rent, as in the case of land acquisition in the different states of India) and subsequent concentration of the newly created rights in the hands of global capital. This is quite similar to the primitive imperial project of occupying territories to take possession of resources. The 'resources' have changed. It does include land and natural resources, but the current phase lays greater emphasis on the occupation of the sites of knowledge production and assimilation, of information and technology, of markets. All these strengthen the rentier character of global capital. The rent is often concealed in profit. The rule of the rentier is concealed in the rule of capital. What are actually payments appropriated by dint of real or imposed immobility of non reproducable resources or conditions of production and sales, are perceived as payment for intellectual effort or for other effort that the prevalent mainstream culture (which also informs the perceptions of the oppressed) thinks to be necessary and so justified. Royalty payments are an example of such payments. While a lot of the literature emphasises the need for providing incentives for innovation through royalties, there is little empirical substantiation of the claim that incentive payments enhance the rate of innovation.[4] In any case the inventor is generally a paid employee, so that the payment is appropriated by the capitalist enterprise that employs the inventor somewhat like a wageworker. Masking rent extraction as 'efficiency price' ensures that such payments appear to be 'rational'. This enhances their legitimacy in the eyes of the intellectuals. This is a typical process through which the existing order persuades one to think of it as *the* superior order. This is an illustration of the process of production of cultural domination through a process that has been termed *synthetic hegemony*.[5] *Hegemony* is the process through which the ruling order attains the consent of the ruled. The particular process of achieving acceptability that we have discussed has been named *synthetic* because the structure masks the ruling order and so makes it acceptable. For example, rent that is derived from the exercise of almost feudal power is accounted mostly as profit that is derived through the working of the 'free capitalist market'. Sometimes it is designated as a different category, royalty, as we have mentioned. But, whatever the designation, it is always considered to be an 'efficiency' price, without which the market mechanism for allocation of resources would not be able to function as a well-oiled machine. In this age of globalisation, the culture of both the dominated and the dominating have internalised the logic of the market. The free market system is perceived to be both self-sufficient and the best system. Even most of the established 'communist' parties prostrate themselves before the inevitability and wisdom of the market. For those of us who are not familiar with the way that the discipline presents the case for freedom of markets, some elaboration is in order.

One of the principal rhetorical strategies that have evolved to sustain the hegemony of the global order of the present age is the deification of the free market as the most efficient system for the solution of economic problems of a society. It has become almost a religious imperative that textbooks of economics must begin by 'proving' to the student that free market is the best thing that could have happened to humanity. Consider, for example, a standard introductory textbook of economics, *Principles of Economics* by Lipsey and Chrystal. I am quoting from the ninth edition:

> Karl Marx argued [in contrast to Adam Smith who had argued, so the authors claim, that individuals acting in self interest and coordinated through an unfettered market produce the best results for the economy]... that when societies become rich enough they should dispense with the spontaneous social order. They should replace it by a consciously created system, called a command economy, or communism, in which the government plans all of

> the transactions that we have just described, and in so doing, creates a more equal and just distribution of the total output.
>
> Beginning with the USSR in the 1920s, many nations listened to Marx and established systems in which conscious government **central planning** largely replaced the spontaneous order of the free market. ...Then, within the last two decades of the century, governments of one communist country after another abandoned their central planning apparatus. More and more economic transactions and activities were then left to be regulated by the self-organising system of the market. *Seldom has a great social issue been settled with such conclusiveness.*

Adam Smith was right and Karl Marx was wrong. (p.2. Italics added, bold as in the original)

In the opener or whatever, (the authors do not give it any conventional heading) the authors start with the title: **Why Study Economics?** Their reply begins with this point:

> One of the most important events in the first half of the twentieth century was the rise of communism. One of the most important events in the second half of the century was communism's fall.... Economic theories are expressly designed to help us understand the successes (and, where they occur, the failures) of free-market societies.

The authors close any further discussion about the contending ways of constructing economic theories *and of contesting power* (in society) by stating the unquestionable principle that 'economic theories are designed to understand the success (and failures...) of free-market societies'. And look how far they extend their rhetoric: not just 'the successes.... of free-market *economies*' but 'of free-market *societies*'. To persuade, they use various ruses: 'success' remains in the body of the text while 'failures' is relegated to a comparatively unimportant existence within a parenthesis. The subtle message is that markets generally perform their task successfully. Another instance of rhetoric that they employ is more difficult to grasp for those trained and indoctrinated in the ways of argument of neoclassical economics, which these two authors pass of as 'economic theories' as such, whose 'express' purpose is to 'understand the successes (and, where they occur, the failures) of free-market societies'. We will frequently have occasion to look back at such argument throughout the course of the book, so if it appears to be dense at this point there is no reason to despair. We are talking of the rhetoric that is unavoidably present in every theory by virtue of the fact that every theory has its own method of proof of what is logical and what is not. This is related to the larger questions of epistemology, of metaphysics. Let us elaborate.

By epistemology is meant a particular branch of philosophy that deals with the question of how to obtain knowledge of the world around us. On a related plain, it also deals, sometimes, with the question of whether it is at all possible to obtain 'true' knowledge of reality. If there are different notions of what constitutes knowledge, then there are bound to be differences regarding criteria of judging what is proper knowledge and what is not. So, every theory tries to convince the reader or listener that its criteria of judgement are the best criteria. For this, it has to use rhetorical devices or means of persuasion. The attempt to establish the metaphysical assumptions of a particular theory as the only proper metaphysical assumption is one of the most important of such rhetorical devices. Metaphysics of a theory is the set of basic and unquestionable assumptions (usually unstated in social sciences) on which the whole theory stands. For example, the nature of agency is a metaphysical assumption of any social science theory. Let us elucidate this point by referring back to our two authors.

> By following their own *self-interest*, doing what seems best and most profitable to *themselves*, and responding to the incentives of prices set by the open markets, people produce a spontaneous social order. (Ibid, p. 1, italics added)

The metaphysical assumption that is unstated (and so rendered invisible, therefore more persuasive) is that the agency of action in the economy is the free, independent individual. This is as much of a doctrinaire assumption as any. If we simply look at the way that advertisements intrude into our decision making, we see how unfounded this assumption is. That is, even without going into the profound questions of the place of subjectivity, its various interpretations and its epistemological status.

Orthodox economics treats the task of proving the superiority of the free market economy with the devotion demanded of a religious mission. To a large extent it succeeds in its task. Consider the innumerable times that we have heard the shopkeeper tell us that he sympathises with our predicament, but what can he do? The market has increased the price. And we have been more or less resigned to this scientific law. There is a general acceptance of the neoclassical claim that the free market is the best economic system. This faith is something that has to be challenged if we are to form any objective view of the process of globalisation. This is one of the things that we have attempted throughout the book.

There is one significant difference between capitalism of this period compared to the earlier incarnations, which needs to be mentioned at the outset, and this has implications for the relation of imperialism with the new postcolonial spaces. Capital is truly global. This implies that the fraction of Indian capital that is a part of global capital has the same aspirations as the rest. For various, generally historical reasons this fraction is not a significant part of global capital. If and when it acquires this stature, Indians can truly feel proud that their nation belongs to the big league of imperialists! But there will be less cause for cheer for the man in the street than there was for the average British, when the plunder of India could fuel an industrial revolution in Britain, and the markets of India were forced to generate demand for British industry. Whatever be the source of global capital, its objectives will remain unchanged. Indian labour will be kept immobile to facilitate rent extraction. Of course, there will be some enclave development, some 'world class' housing for the rich, some golf courses. So, the problems of unemployment and poverty will remain as acute as ever even if our state becomes a respectable imperial state. One has only to observe the continuing distress of the common Chinese in spite of that country's much-touted growth.

The logic is simple. Our huge population is the key. In spite of the vast multitude living and dying below the official poverty level, even a small fraction of the population with incomes sufficient to indulge in luxuries constitutes a phenomenal absolute number of buyers. Already the indications are there. A striking recent example of the power of this market that comes to mind is the sea change that has been brought about in the organisation and even the very fibre of the game of cricket by the wealth of the Board of Cricket Control of India (BCCI), which is based on the mind-boggling numbers that view televised cricket matches in India. This television audience includes a large number of potential buyers of the luxury items that are advertised throughout the matches. Advertisement charge is the source of revenue for those television channels that buy exclusive telecasting rights from the BCCI. These companies therefore pay phenomenal amounts to procure telecast rights. This funds the riches of BCCI and now of the Khans and Mallyas investing in the various teams that will fight it out like gladiators in the Indian Premier League (IPL). Obviously the mercenaries will have to be well paid. But the point is that the face of the game will soon be changed beyond recognition. It will no longer be a game where teams battle it out for national glory. It will be a game in which hired players fight it out for attaining greater individual market value. In all this, the Board of Cricket Control of a particular nation will call all the shots, making the International Cricket Council (ICC) a titular head, much in the way that the USA has rendered the UNO a figurehead. Look, we are not judging. In fact, this process goes some way towards tearing the 'feudal...idyllic relations.... and has left remaining no other nexus between man and man than naked self-interest, than callous "cash payment". It has drowned the most heavenly ecstasies of religious fervour, of chivalrous enthusiasm, of philistine sentimentalism, in the icy water of egotistical calculation.' (Marx, 1969) And one may say that it has also drowned the fervour of patriotism. We just want to point out the potential that our nation has to join the big league and to indicate the source of this strength.

Though the purpose of this book is to excite the reader to think about the structure of globalisation, we have not laid equal emphasis on all aspects. Our focus has been on the international economic organisations – the World Bank, International Monetary Fund (IMF) and the World Trade Organisation (WTO).

The conditions imposed by these institutions on their members, and the changes that have occurred in these conditions over the years, reveal the changing face of capital in the post-Second World War situation. We do not pretend to present a comprehensive picture of the working of these organisations, though we have dealt in some detail with the organisational and administrative structure of these bodies.

Along with our understanding of what globalisation is all about, we have also talked of our vision of an alternative course of development, though in a rather sketchy manner. The vision is not radically new, but one that we have chosen to forget. It is that of 'construction and struggle'. Put simply, this position advocates that the struggle against the suffocating order of global capital can be articulated only if it is supplemented with a positive programme of construction (both material and moral) through *community* effort. This conception of struggle, which is rooted in the ideas of nationalists like Tagore and Gandhi as much as it is in the ideas of the Marxist revolutionary, Shankar Guha Neogi, is a little deceptive in its apparent simplicity. For one thing, the community that we have referred to will itself be defined through the process of construction and struggle. We will elaborate upon these ideas in Chapter 8. The outline that we present there will have to be filled in. And perceptions of struggle and construction can be redrawn in the course of discussions and practice. My purpose will have been served if the book can in any way provoke this process.

I will end the introductory chapter by pointing to a difference in the method of exposition of this volume from other attempts to conceptualise the current global scenario that are written from some leftist position. Typically, such ventures announce their originality by highlighting their differences with other leftist analyses. Inevitably therefore, these expositions are replete with criticism of other left positions. Though we have not completely abjured such critiques, our arguments are mainly presented through critiques of the neoclassical position or the orthodox defence of the current global order. This approach is explained mainly by the history of this tract. Most of the book was written as a series of articles motivated by the desire to make the man on the street aware of the long-term economic and consequent cultural debility that globalisation is causing: specifically, the violence that it breeds. It was felt, in this context, that the more urgent need was to equip the reader with critiques of the ruling defences of globalisation rather than with highlighting differences among self-proclaimed left positions. In the concluding chapter we have spelt out some of our differences with other left positions.

NOTES

1. This school, which publishes the journal *Rethinking Marxism*, subscribes to the anti-essentialist position that all social processes influence each other to build what they call, not in a very expressive way, an overdetermined social totality. (This term was not invented by this group and has gained currency since the French Marxist philosopher, Luis Althusser, employed it.) But the thickly woven social texture is impenetrable in its dense reality. So, to analytically delve into it, they approach the reality from a particular perspective, which they call, vividly, the epistemological entry point. Their position can be explicated from various articles in the mentioned journal. The most comprehensive articulation is to be found in 'Knowledge and Class' (Resnick, S.A. and Wolf, A.R., 1987).
2. This was co-authored by Ajit Chaudhury, Dipankar Das and Anjan Chakraborty (Chaudhury A., Das D. and Chakraborty A., 2000). The notion of *mimicry of overdetermination*, which was first presented there and which we deploy later, has blossomed in somewhat divergent ways in the writings of Chaudhury and Das, which, unfortunately for the English reader, has not been translated from Bengali, in which they were written.
3. This is a payment that is extracted on the basis of monopoly rights over a resource that is either non reproducable or restrictions over the mobility of which introduce an element of regional non reproducability of the resource. We will elaborate on this idea as we go along.
4. Dubey, M., 1992.
5. The notion of synthetic hegemony was developed by Chaudhury (1988).

2

Globalisation in a Different Sense

In one sense, all right-thinking people support globalisation. If globalisation means disseminating the sense of global citizenship, extending cross-cultural dialogue while maintaining cultural identities; increasing global exchange without curbing local sovereignty, then we are all for it.

But, from the seventies of the last century, 'globalisation' is being used in a specific, narrow sense. This new globalisation or the global system has, apparently, only one demand from nation states: decrease the power of governments to influence economic decisions, leaving this to the markets. Of course, if this principle goes against the interests of any rich nation, it is easily sacrificed.[1] In practice, therefore, 'globalisation' apparently means taking away the rights of the governments of the poor countries to intervene in their domestic economies or in international trade. But even this is a rather superficial position. It is true that the governments of rich nations have the latitude to take some decisions that may affect global capital adversely, a freedom that is denied to the governments of the poor countries. But, as we will argue in detail later, it is a myth assiduously cultivated by mainstream academia, and spread in degenerate forms by the media, that the 'market economy' stands on self-sufficient scientific rules. The global capitalist market system is founded on state violence aimed at dispossession of communities to make resources like land, nature and even community knowledge private, marketable commodities. This simultaneously makes the dispossessed communities the refugees of development. Within the dominant culture, this process of dispossession appears as a logical outcome of the working of the dynamics of the market.[2] The rebellious peasant or the forest dependent people, who do not 'see' this logic, are simply dubbed as irrational and disruptive. The most that sympathy towards them will elicit from the ruling parties is the plea that they should be educated about the need for such dispossession.[3] Thus the governments, of the rich countries undoubtedly but even those of poor countries, are in fact playing a more aggressive role in the restructuring of property rights in the service of (global) capital than in the preceding period.

We will attempt to analyse the components of this pervasive phenomenon called globalisation that are themselves articulated in the process. Like all other commentators, we will view the process from a particular vantage position. We do not think that any discussion of society can be free of bias. Those who claim 'neutrality' and 'scientificity' in support of their position are simply trying to dupe others. To be fair, their analysis is often so shallow, that they themselves are fooled into this belief. Our point of view is a working peoples' point of view. By this we mean that we are principally concerned with the mechanism of production of surplus and its appropriation. But the position is not dogmatic. As will become evident in due course, we are as much interested in the state of those who are disinherited by the process of development and temporarily, at least, excluded from the process of exploitation. We will try to understand globalisation from a position, which believes that all have a right to food, clothing and shelter; from a position, which has the faith that it is unethical to seize common rights over natural resources. Overriding such 'elementary aspects' is our faith that any acceptable path of development can only emerge out of a participatory process. It cannot be an imposed path. But this anticipates the position that we have reached partly as a result of the process of evolution of this book.

Post-Second World War

We will have to dig a little into the past to get a historical perspective, which is essential for understanding the current world economy. We have to go back at least to the period immediately succeeding the Second World War, because the international economic agencies that are today pressurising the governments of the poor countries to adopt anti-people policies, or their predecessors, were born during this era.

Europe was devastated by war. Partly in order to put their houses in order, and partly on account of the pressure exerted by the USA, a kind of unanimity emerged among the Western countries regarding the proper attitude of the government of a country towards its economy. Broadly, the countries that could influence opinion at international forums felt that government had to intervene in a planned manner in the domestic economy to tackle the problems of unemployment, lack of social security, low production, etc. At the same time, they were generally opposed to government intervention in international exchange.

This apparent consensus was a rather fragile understanding. One strand of economic theory was used to support the suggested set of domestic policies and a completely opposite strand to support the set of international policies. The theoretical ideas of the British Finance Minister, John Maynard Keynes (which is called Keynesian economics) were used to support the suggested domestic policies, and classical economic ideas were used to argue in favour of the proposed policies in the sphere of international exchange. The inherent contradictions between the Keynesian and classical views indicate the fragility of the understanding. Actually, if one supports government intervention in the domestic economy, one can in no way champion free international exchange. Let us explain this contention.

Nowadays we often hear that subsidies will have to be reduced in various sectors. This is a condition imposed by the WTO. Their argument is that if a domestic producer is subsidised, the producer will be able to sell at prices lower than that of international competitors. This reduces domestic competition. Again, in place of subsidy, if the government opts for an alternative to subsidy, that is, government purchases domestically manufactured products, their demand rises. As a result the rate of inflation may increase temporarily. In that case the demand for domestically manufactured goods declines in the international market. The demand for imports that substitute domestic products in the home market rises. Deficit occurs in the balance of payments. In this situation, if the government does not have the right to intervene in international transactions, there may be a crisis caused by depletion of foreign exchange reserves. So, intervention in the domestic economy by the government of a country amounts to interference in international exchange (as elaborated in the case of subsidisation of domestic producer by the government) or it must be directly supplemented by intervention by the government in international trade and payments (as in the case of government purchase of domestically-produced wares).

Capital has no particular love for either classical or Keynesian principles. It is only the theoreticians who have vested interests in crying hoarse for this or that school. Why should the capitalist object if the state provides subsidies or if the state purchases what capital makes? But, subsidising one sector may fuel demands for subsidising other sectors, and this may ultimately go against the originally subsidised sector. If capital is subsidised, other classes may demand that the government intervene to their benefit. It may not be possible to reject such demands within a democratic set-up. Capitalists decide the quantity and type of concessions they should demand from the government after taking into account many such considerations.[4]

The governments of the rich countries work in the overall interests of capital. But its interests have to be defended within a particular historical and geographical context. For example, let us assume that the capitalists stand to gain a lot if the Minimum Wages Act is scrapped. But whether the government will be able to abolish the Act or not will depend on the organisational strength of the workers. Keynesian theory says that additional income is generated if the government steps up its expenditure. A share of this income is spent to buy consumer goods. So demand rises again. Production and income increase. In this way income keeps rising successively. This theory is completely silent about the heads under which government expenditure is to increase. Even if the government decides to help capital through Keynesian policies, the relative strengths of the different class organisations or organisations of economic agents with more or less homogeneous interests determine the direction in which expenditure will flow. The government can increase social welfare spending, i.e. subsidies to education or for healthcare. Or it can grant differential tax concessions to various segments, depending on their relative political clout. Just as what the state can do domestically to help capital depends on the relative strengths of the pressure groups within the nation, the competitive position of national capital (or, to shed some of the traditional connotations of this term, capital sourced within the nation) in the international sphere determines feasible state policy in the international arena.

When the USA was championing the cause of free trade most vociferously, immediately after the Second World War, it was also the most active in keeping agricultural products outside the purview of free trade regulations. The reason was that the American farmer would have been swept away by international competition if its doors were opened to free imports of agricultural commodities.

International Agreements

As a result of these various pulls and pushes after the Second World War, the rich nations came to some sort of an agreement that within a nation the sovereign state should have the authority to formulate economic policies independently, while in the sphere of international exchange there should be a gradual move towards free markets. These nations were, however, no moralist sticklers for principles. Whenever they have felt the need they have violated these principles without being burdened with any guilt whatever and they have also cajoled and persuaded the concerned international organisations into giving these deviations their stamp of approval. An early example of such double dealing is the successful efforts of the

USA to keep agriculture out of the purview of The General Agreement on Trade and Tariff (GATT).

An agreement was signed at Bretton Woods in 1944, on the basis of the broad consensus reached between the rich nations that we have just referred to. Following this agreement, the World Bank and the IMF were set up. The World Bank began functioning in 1946 and the IMF in 1947. Simultaneously, the decision to set up an international trade body was taken at a bilateral meeting between the USA and Britain in 1945. On the basis of this understanding, an international conference was convened at Havana in 1948 by the United Nations Organisation (UNO). This conference decided to set up an International Trade Organisation (ITO). But, because the American Senate refused to endorse the agreement, a loose coordination, called the General Agreement on Trade and Tariff (GATT) emerged on the basis of the Havana Agreement.

The World Bank was initially created to reconstruct war-devastated Europe. Later the Bank started extending loans to poor countries, largely directed at specific projects. It was the responsibility of the IMF to bring stability to the exchange rates between the currencies of the member countries. The Fund was also entrusted with the responsibility of extending short-term loans to member countries in order to prevent sudden fluctuations in exchange rates. The GATT was successively modified through rounds of Multilateral Trade Negotiations (MTNs). Its task was, mainly, to promote liberalisation of trade in goods, without hampering the interests of rich nations.

Rich Country – Poor Country

There was an unstable equilibrium in the period following the Second World War. This was based, as we have mentioned, on two major principles: not to intervene explicitly, in the power of the sovereign states to formulate policies with regard to the domestic economy, and to move progressively towards liberalisation of trade in the international market, taking care, of course, not to hamper the interests of rich nations in any significant way. However, in a garbed way, the economic sovereignty of many poor countries was being traded off even before the 1970s. During the 1960s many underdeveloped nations, including India, were forced to devalue[5] their currencies under pressure from the rich nations and the international economic organisations controlled by them. A country is not one monolithic entity. There are various classes and groups. Like so many other questions, the degree of sovereignty a nation enjoys is decided through conflicts, pressures and counter-pressures among the various social agglomerations, groups and collectives. Such conflicts are compounded by international contradictions. The conscious worker, that is the one who thinks of this problem, would want the sovereignty of the nation to remain unsullied. It is almost impossible for a worker to convey one's dissent or protest or to influence policy in any way, if the power to control livelihood resides abroad. Rules relating to security of jobs, minimum wage laws, social security, all become mired in uncertainty. But such general concerns do not motivate the entire working class. For example, in today's world a small segment of the working class employed in MNCs, particularly those in the service sector, hypnotised by the high salaries become disinterested in the question of national sovereignty (till it is too late!). The indigenous capitalist class is not predisposed in favour of, or against, national sovereignty as opposed to the interests of the MNCs. (Also, such conflict exists only between fractions of national capital that have not been globalised and globalised capital.) Calculations of expected profit and loss determine which way they will swing. The contradictions between the classes and class fractions, and the degree of international pressure that a nation can withstand determine when and to what extent sovereignty will be traded off.

Rule of Dollar and Devaluation

The fragile agreement that had been reached among the rich nations after the Second World War began to crumble from the 1970s. The USA had lost its pre-eminent position as the leader of the rich capitalist nations. After Bretton Woods, the dollar had been accepted as the major medium of international transactions. If I can print dollar notes and can compel all to accept these notes in payment of transactions, then I do not have to earn any money. I can print money and buy to my heart's desire. Again, since these notes are widely used for transactions, their demand also increases over time. Up to the 1970s this was the position enjoyed by the USA. First the war-devastated nations of Europe were dependent on the USA for their reconstruction. Later the capitalist world became almost subservient to America as it was recognised as the general who led the 'free world' in its declared and undeclared wars against the socialist world. So, America could not only run up huge deficits on its balance of payments, it was even encouraged to do so.

By the 1970s this need began to diminish. Japan and the European nations emerged as competitors of America, with very strong economies of their own. America was not proving to be as redoubtable a leader of the 'free world' as had been imagined. Remember, these were the dying years of the Vietnamese War. Under these circumstances, the nations, which were contending with USA for international economic power, no longer thought that it was necessary to accept the dollar as *the* medium of international exchange. The USA could not run up deficits in its balance of payments at will. The Frank, Mark and Yen became quite acceptable in payment for international transactions. In the attempt to reduce the balance of payments deficit, the dollar was devalued (which was in violation of the Bretton Woods agreement). Thus without any declaration, the agreement was abandoned.

Free Capital Flows

Around this time, certain new tendencies emerged in the international economy. The MNCs began to show interest in transferring the labour-intensive parts of production processes to the poor countries, in search of cheap labour. As a result, productive[6] and speculative[7] capital felt the need to expand the field of international circulation. Capital's desire to expand into new areas was later accelerated by the emergence of the new information technology. It is now possible to transmit information and commands from one corner of the globe to another instantly and almost at no cost. Consequently, on the one hand, the large factory organisations are being broken up and fragments put out to small producers in the manner of dependent petty production before the industrial revolution. On the other hand, there is also a tendency to export specific parts of the process abroad. At least one political implication of these tendencies is significant. Because the workers do not work together, trade unions become weak.

The USA began to lag behind in technology for manufacturing goods. It realised that in the changed circumstances, it had a comparative advantage in the supply of financial services, like banking and insurance. The USA began actively searching for newer ways to expand the international market for these commodities. Simultaneously, to compensate for the loss on account of its outdated technology in the manufacturing sector, it was looking to expand the scope of rent earning by appropriating and establishing rights over intellectual properties, life forms and such other unexplored territories. At the same time, the move towards globalisation of capital, in the sense of the loss of significance of national origin of capital, began to gain momentum. This was to become a key issue, as we will discuss later.

The effectiveness of the new policies in achieving the desired objectives depends to a large extent on the degree to which global capital can control the economies of the host countries. Global finance capital[8] needs to ensure total freedom of entry and exit. Because of its pronounced speculative character, it requires a legal and administrative environment, which allows easier and faster mobility than that required by global capital rooted in production. It must also be ensured that the laws of the host country do not impose any restriction on its manner of functioning within that country. Laws, regulations, and fiscal policies of the host must be prevented from discriminating against global capital. It also became necessary to expand the scope of GATT to bring trade in services within its scope. Finally, laws relating to patents and other properties had to be changed and standardised so as to allow global capital the power to acquire rights over knowledge and 'natural resources', including life forms.

The necessary changes were introduced from the 1970s through the aggressive intervention of IMF and World Bank, and from the 1990s through the efforts of the WTO, which was the successor of GATT. From the 1970s the World Bank and the IMF started interfering in the domestic policy making of the borrower countries on the pretext of ensuring that the loans were being properly utilised. The 1980s saw these organisations interfere more openly. The borrower countries became contractually bound to allow such interference through the Structural Adjustment Programme and the Stabilisation Programme. The ultimate step in the abrogation of economic sovereignty of the poor countries was taken in 1994 with the formation of the WTO. We will discuss its structure and mode of operation in detail in later chapters, but it would not be amiss at this point to mention that this was the first agreement whereby changes in economic laws approved by an international organisation became binding on the members, after a certain period, even without the approval of its legislature and its judicial system. Of course, the WTO, like its predecessor GATT, has allowed various exemptions keeping in mind the interests of the rich nations. For instance, it has kept the international flow of workers in search of jobs outside its scheme of liberalisation.

This, in summary form, is the historical background to globalisation. In the following chapters we will discuss in some detail the organisational, political, and economic aspects of the international economic organisations to elaborate upon our view that 'globalisation', as it is currently used, is nothing more than a period of aggressive search for new territories by global capital. ('Territory' here does not just refer to geographical space, but also to other conceptual spaces like the space of knowledge.) We will end this short road map of globalisation (which, like all maps, has a definite intention built into its construction) with our embryonic dreams of an alternative globalisation, tracing also the antecedents of this dream.

NOTES

1. 'Multinational corporations continue to be rooted in states. The biggest have half their assets, markets and labour forces located in a single home state, to which they look to protect their interests. Capitalism can no more do without the state today than it could in the Keynesian period. State intervention has been used to drive through attacks on workers, as with Margaret Thatcher's antiunion laws or the use of the police against the miners' strike of 1984-5. But it has also repeatedly been used to protect sections of capital against the effects of crisis in a way supposedly ruled out by neoliberal ideology. The US state helped bail out Chrysler when it came close to going bust in 1979; it took charge of negotiations in the 1980s to prevent US banks being dragged under by unpayable debts from Latin American countries. In 1998 it propped up the Long Term Capital Management hedge fund and, most recently, through the Federal Reserve central bank, it has tried to limit the damage caused to the financial system by the subprime mortgage crisis. Indeed, states have intervened more to deal with crises since the 1970s than in the 1960s and 1950s for the simple reason that the crises have been much more severe.' Chris Harman; 'Theorising neoliberalism'; *International Socialism*, Issue: 117.
2. This was always a crucial part of bourgeois apology for capitalism. As Marx writes:

   'This primitive accumulation plays approximately the same role in political economy as original sin does in theology. Adam bit the apple, and thereupon sin fell on the human race. Its origin is supposed to be explained when it is told as an anecdote about the past. Long, long ago there were two sorts of people; one the diligent, intelligent, and above all frugal elite; the other lazy rascals, spending their substance, and more, in riotous living. The legend of theological original sin tells us certainly how man came to be condemned to eat his bread by the sweat of his brow; but the history of economic original sin reveals to us that there are people to whom this is by no means essential.

   Never mind! Thus it came to pass that the former sort accumulated wealth, and the latter sort finally had nothing to sell except their own skins.' (Marx, K., 1954:667)
3. At a recent seminar an economist, who is well known in West Bengal, had repeated the well-worn arguments of the ruling Left Front about the absolute need for industrialisation and therefore, for acquisition of agricultural land. When asked by a participant

whether it was the felt need of the dispossessed, the chairperson, who is a nationally well-known economist, tried to appropriate the question and the questioner by 'agreeing' that the peasants had to be educated. The two positions, of course, became irreconciliable when the interlocutor interjected that he had meant to ask who had given the right to the economists like the presenter to decide for the potential oustees.

4. That is not to say that the process is some kind of mathematical exercise with the outcomes of the options available being totally predictable to the capitalists. Nor do we mean to suggest that capitalists sit together at their federations or chambers of industries and decide these issues as a well-knit body. There definitely are parleys on such issues at their associations. But there are also differences of interests among the capitalists on these issues. Particularly, many of the fractions of capital find it more directly profitable and easier to persuade the government if they demand discriminatory subsidies on specific grounds, than if they demand that the government should not subsidise other segments of the population or that the government should extend across the board subsidies to the entire capitalist sector. But, to write a sentence describing this process without assigning decision making to any individual or class position would reduce readability considerably. Without going directly into all the weighty questions of the functional (real life) significance of classes versus discursive (expressed in words in the course of a discussion) significance, we would say in defence of such grammatical construction that if we were to go into all the deconstructive riders to each subject position (that is one who is portrayed to be in the decision-making position) then we would not be able to proceed in any readable manner. (Now 'readability' becomes a vehicle of imposing the dominant ideological position regarding the subject of social action! And so we would go on and on. This is quite predictable within the post-modern way of thinking: supplements generate further supplements in an endless process). We could say perhaps more precisely and less readably (!) that how much the capitalist demands is the outcome of the interaction of structural causality of the system and an indeterminate degree of voluntary action of the capitalists and the reactions which are similarly determined. But the problem would not end there as indeed it never will – just as all action, all choice is always in process – so also is all 'proper' description of these.

5. Devaluation here means the reduction in the announced price of the domestic currency in terms of foreign exchange. This can happen only in a regime where the rates of exchange (i.e. the price of domestic currency in terms of foreign currencies) are fixed by the central banks, and not freely determined by the market. In case the market determines the foreign exchange rate, the government or the central monetary authority does not announce any exchange rate.
6. Capital, which is invested in the production of goods and services. It is always related to the transformation of the inputs purchased by this capital.
7. This capital is not used for purchasing inputs for their transformation. Its sole source of profit is buying cheap and selling dear. In the specific context, which we are discussing, such purchase and resale is restricted mainly to financial papers, like shares, and currencies of nations. This capital is more mobile than productive capital. That is, it can move out of one geographical region (or sector) and into another region or sector, more easily than productive capital can. In this context another similar couple may be mentioned: direct investment and portfolio investment. If capital is spent to buy land to set up an enterprise, say, the money spent would be counted as direct investment and the land acquired would be reckoned as productive capital. The land may be sold off and the capital, which is released from this venture, may be invested in some other enterprise. But this is a time-consuming affair. If money were instead invested in the purchase of shares, the expenditure on shares would be called portfolio investment and the shares acquired would be counted as speculative capital. The term 'portfolio' refers to the portfolio in which the share papers used to be stored. The significance, probably, is that the portfolio moves with its owner. Such investment is called speculative because shares are normally purchased if the buyer speculates, or anticipates that the price of the share is likely to rise in future. The intention behind such purchase is to sell off for a gain once the price rises. The shares can be sold and the money, which was invested, can be moved to some other investment site with much greater ease than is the case with the capital, which was invested in land.
8. The term is used in a sense that is synonymous to the sense in which the term 'speculative capital' has been used in this chapter. 'Speculative capital' is a broader term and can refer to speculation in both tangible goods as well as in financial papers and

currencies, but, as we have noted, in the current phase of the international economy, international speculation is restricted almost entirely to the speculation in the latter. Definitionally, though, the term is used to distinguish investment in various kinds of papers or promissory notes from investment in, say, land. The latter kind of investment (i.e. investment in property which has intrinsic usefulness) is called real investment. The former (i.e. investment in property which has no usefulness of its own) is referred to as a financial investment.

3

The International Monetary Fund: The Harsh Ethics of Global Capital

A Theoretical Perspective

There cannot, as we have already stated, be a neutral viewpoint. One looks at 'reality' from a particular position, or maybe, a complex and worrying combination of positions, of which one may, or may not, always be fully aware. There are no exceptions. Our analysis of globalisation stands in a particular theoretical field. We do not, of course, suggest that our perspective or field of concepts is able to picture the 'reality' of globalisation, either, in a self-contained manner. This is a post-modern commonplace, and it is also an unavoidable position if the chosen theoretical perspective is to allow any significance to experience, to the practice of the activist.

We agree with the criticism that the left parties and political groups in India have not given much thought to the evolution/ mutation of imperialism through the latter half of the twentieth century. But we think that the malaise is much deeper. One has hardly thought about what a left approach or position means; let alone think of a leftist approach to New Imperialism. Marxists generally use dominant, bourgeois (or, shall we say, marketable) categories of economic analysis. To show their allegiance to Marxism, they spruce up their writings with some jargon, which have a well-established Marxist lineage. It is not just the political practitioners who suffer from with this lack of criticality, but left academics too suffer from this simple-mindedness. Or is it so simple!

We agree with the view that Lenin's **Imperialism the Highest Stage of Capitalism** was written with a particular historical-political crossroads of crisis in mind. The focus was on the contradiction or conflict of interest between the imperialist countries and the resultant possibility of a world war. He was concerned with the task of the working class in this situation. In the present-day context such contradiction, to the extent that it exists, is of little consequence to the workers in the third world. In fact, our major thesis is that globalisation involves, among other things, the loss of national identity of capital. In a summary fashion, one may say that globalisation is the campaign launched by globalised capital (i.e. big capital or capital which has crossed a certain threshold size, which makes it eligible to the benefits of global mobility) to secure rights over natural resources, stock of common knowledge, and markets of the third world in order to extract rent. Against this campaign the third world people are organising to defend their local rights (traditional common rights) and rights of access to markets. In this process of resistance, they are defining new communities every moment. This is the principal contradiction of capitalism today: that between the local and the global. We will discuss the evolution of the international economic organisations in the light of this conflict. This focus provokes the question as to which side national capital belongs. Or, more fundamentally, whether one can at all define such a category today. The so-called national bourgeois displays its vacillating character prominently in this age of financial and technical collaboration and mobility. Sometimes it is a part of the broad front that tries to prevent further sell-out of sovereignty of the nation, sometimes it becomes a defender of the need for further opening up of the economy. It all depends on its anticipations about the possible impact of such policy changes on its profitability. Also, there is a host of small capitalists whose existence is threatened by the aggressive expansionism of the MNCs. In spite of these riders and some degree of unpredictability in the behaviour pattern of the capitalists, reflecting political caprice, we would generally tend to concur with the view that it is now no longer possible to rely on national capital for building an alternative production system that can stand up against the exploitation of national resources by global capital. The very concept of national capital has lost its significance other than as a strategic slogan that can be used by certain fractions of large capital to further their own competitive interests. Acquisition of Corus steel by Tatas has no significance for the working people of India but they manage to win some sort of national approval and backing for their 'victory'. The working people have to invent alternative productive organisations here and now. Experimenting with worker's cooperatives is one way of working towards an alternative.

One must not think of such exploration as a sort of competition between different forms of production organisations. It must be a part of the effort of construction of both the dream of 'socialist construction' and the construction of socialist ethos – the construction of consciousness. A figure that one must recall here, not as a *guru*, but because his call 'construct and struggle' can serve as a short hand for a lot of things we wish to say, is that of Shankar Guha Neogi. Though the ideas, which continue to excite us, emerged from the experience of the movement of the tribal population of Chhattisgarh, (so the patent should vest with them!) Shankar Guha Neogi collated, and compared critically and contextually, these experiences and drew the conclusion that one must combine construction and struggle in the course of a movement. We will talk about all this in greater detail in Chapter 8.

When one says that there is a great gulf between the imperialism of today and that of Lenin's time, one often proposes implicitly that the significance of the state has diminished greatly in this new era of globalisation. A different withering away of the state![1] It is true that the flexibility of the state, particularly in economic matters, is being gradually eroded, especially in the poor countries, through the process of liberalisation. But this does not mean that the need for state power has been exhausted. In fact, what probably differentiates this age of imperialism from its immediate predecessor (that is the period extending right up to the 60s and 70s of the last century) is its immense dependence on state power for rewriting economic laws and for their harsh implementation. In the previous period – which used to be called the period of neo-imperialism – imperialist capital's open and observable reliance on the state was not the order of the day, while in the present era laws, regulations, and even principles of jurisprudence are being grossly altered with impunity to facilitate imperialist plunder. In this overt fight the international economic organisations play a stellar and crucial role, but it is only through state power, modified to suit the needs of global capital that the necessary changes can be implemented. So the contention that the importance of state power is vanishing, wittingly or unwittingly, aids global capital's 'feudal'[2] plunder.

A concept that is central to our analysis of the international economic organisations, is 'Primitive Capital Accumulation' (PCA). It may be helpful to the reader if we present, at this point, our reading of this process and the reason why we consider it to be of central importance in discussing the political economy of globalisation. Since the demise of the primitive tribal communities,[3] society has been divided into the surplus-producing working classes and the surplus-appropriating classes. In each society surplus is appropriated in a specific set of ways that are internally coherent. For a particular mode of appropriation to be viable, a spectrum of state structures, containing a particular concept of legality at its core, is necessary. The modern capitalist state and its legal system may appear to be non-discriminatory because, in a formal sense, they are impersonal. The capitalist has the necessary finances to purchase the inputs, including labour power, which is required for production. The laws of private property ensure that the inputs belong to the capitalist because he/she has purchased it in the market. So the output produced from these inputs also belong to the capitalist. The money earned by selling this final product in the market constitutes the revenue of the capitalist. The excess of the revenue over the cost of purchase of the inputs is the surplus, which, naturally belongs to the capitalist. So, for appropriating surplus, as profit, all that seems to be necessary is that the market should function.

Market is the place where exchange of goods and services occurs. In an act of exchange, two parties simultaneously give and take two properties that are of equal worth. For example, I give ten rupees to the shopkeeper and the shopkeeper gives me a ball-pen. They are of equal worth, in the sense that we have both agreed to this. Otherwise, the transaction would not have taken place. This exchange is possible because I was recognised as the legitimate owner of rupees ten, and the shopkeeper was recognised as the owner of the ball-pen. Also, once the shopkeeper and I had agreed to the price, exchange required that we kept the contract to exchanging the ball-pen and the money. In plain words, it was necessary that I did not run away with the ball-pen when it was handed over to me. Thus, for the market to function only the laws of private property and contract are necessary. These laws are impersonal. Anyone who has the money can own property (the state does not designate by name who can own property). Any two persons who own property can contract to exchange (the state does not bar any property owner from exchanging the property).

But this blasé indifference can be sustained only by a very crude and fundamental discrimination below the surface. This discrimination constitutes a process that is both prior and simultaneous to the working of the 'non-discriminating' capitalist market. The capitalist is able to earn profit through the process of buying and selling in the market, which just requires this neutral state apparatus, only because the working classes have been dispossessed of all means of production other than the ability to labour. This is, of course, a commonplace of Marxism, but one whose deep significance has conveniently been forgotten by many Marxists, particularly those running states, which are trying to curry favour with global capital. How else can one explain the eagerness verging on greed with which a state government run by Marxists is displacing farmers to provide land for setting up industrial ventures, up market housing complexes, and the works.[4] The process of dispossession is an elementary aspect of PCA. There is a widely held view that this process occurs prior to the establishment of capitalism. The seeds of this idea are there in Marx's **Capital.**[5] In reality, this process is endlessly entwined with capital's expansion. Marx discussed the process of dispossession in the context of right to land, but the process of dispossession/ occupation, which is essential to the survival, and expansion of capital can be treated as a theoretical concept. For its expansion, capital does not appropriate just land. It acquires rights over knowledge, culture, nature and even the games that people play. In fact, the process of acquiring control over markets can be seen, theoretically, as a part of PCA. The market constitutes a territory as much as land. On the basis of control over markets, capital appropriates rent, which is concealed as profit. Marx calls this 'surplus profit' and treats it as a kind of absolute rent. (Marx, 1959, p. 775)

The laws of the state and economic rules and regulations are changed, even drastically, whenever necessary to facilitate this war of occupation. The international economic organisations – the IMF, the World Bank, and the newly constituted WTO – have the permanent responsibility of initiating, monitoring and supervising these changes.

The Birth of IMF

The IMF is one of the international institutions that emerged from the Bretton Woods agreement. The professed purposes of the fund were: to bring about stability of exchange rates; to influence central banks of different countries to reduce restrictions on the availability of foreign exchange for current account transactions; to extend short-term loans from the fund's own resources to help members tide over temporary deficits in their balance of payments. The fund was built with the contributions made by members in amounts specified by their respective quotas. The quotas were fixed on the basis of the foreign exchange reserves held by a country, the GNP of the country, the volume of international trade of the country and unstated political considerations. Naturally, the contributions of the rich countries were large.

In a formal sense the Board of Governors manages the fund. There is one governor from each member country. In practice it is run by the Executive Directors. There are thirteen such directors. Of them, five are nominated by the five countries, which have the largest quotas. One is nominated by a country, which has a surplus on its balance of payments. The other countries elect the other seven directors.

The control of the rich countries is more obviously reflected in the distribution of votes. The value of a vote depends on the relative size of the voter's quota. For example, the USA has about twenty per cent of votes, while India has less than three per cent.

This discriminatory system is based on normal capitalist principles. One can think of the IMF as a joint stock commercial bank, with the member countries as shareholders. Naturally, the share of votes controlled by a shareholder will depend on one's proportionate shareholding. The major shareholder, the USA, understandably enjoys certain privileges at the Bank.

The First Phase: US Dominance and Intervention in External Policy

The IMF was established mainly to avoid chaos in international currency exchanges after the Second World War. When a country imports any good or service from some other country it has to pay in foreign exchange. On the other hand, when it exports it earns foreign exchange. Let us elaborate on this process a bit. Suppose a foreigner wants to buy an Indian shirt. The Indian firm that has manufactured the shirt will, obviously, accept payment only in a currency which it can use in its business. This firm has to pay its input suppliers and labour in rupees. So it will demand payment in rupees. The foreigner will have to sell the currency of his/her country to procure the necessary amount of rupees. Thus the exports of India generate a supply of foreign exchange in the international currency market equal to the value of the exports, and an equivalent demand for rupees. Conversely, when an Indian wants to buy a car manufactured abroad, he/she has to pay the foreign manufacture in the currency of the country in which the company is located. The Indian buyer will, therefore, supply an amount of rupees, in the foreign currency market, equal in worth to the foreign currency value of the car. Simultaneously the Indian buyer of the car demands that amount of foreign currency, in the foreign exchange market. In sum, exports generate supply of foreign currency and equivalent demand for domestic currency. On the other hand, imports generate supply of domestic currency and equivalent demand for foreign currency.

There is, therefore, an excess supply of foreign exchange, generated through the international transactions of a country, if it has a surplus of exports over imports (ignoring of course other forms of international exchange). Simultaneously, there is an excess demand for the domestic currency of the country, in the foreign exchange market. In other words, in the market for international currencies, those foreigners intending to import commodities from the home country, offer greater value of foreign currencies in order to purchase the domestic currency of the nation, than is demanded by the importers of foreign commodities in the home country, against sale of domestic currency. In this case, if the exchange rate is unregulated, then the price of the domestic currency in terms of foreign currency (say, $/Re.) should rise, as happens in any unregulated market when there is excess demand for the commodity. Conversely, there should be a tendency for the price of the currency to fall in terms of foreign exchange if the country has a deficit in its balance of trade (i.e. if imports exceed exports).

In the current context, however, one item among what we have ignored turns out to be more important than the trade balance itself. It is the flow of speculative capital.[6] If the exchange rate fluctuates rapidly, producers invariably suffer. The prices of imported inputs and exported output become uncertain. The dollar or pound price of exports declines if the price of the rupee falls, as the price of an export commodity of India is designated in rupee. Conversely, more rupees have to be paid for imports of inputs by the Indian manufacturer, the price of such inputs being given in some foreign currency. The currency speculators may, however gain from the fluctuations, depending on their accuracy in predicting the fluctuations.

There was little speculative activity in the international currency market at the time the IMF was formed. No powerful capitalist lobby stood to gain from sudden changes in the exchange rates. Hence, keeping exchange rates stable became the principal objective of the IMF. The IMF tried to maintain a fixed exchange rate system more or less up to the end of the 1960s. The Central Bank of a country could change the value of its currency. But the IMF had to be informed in advance, and once announced, the Central Bank had to maintain that rate. Going back to our simple example, if a country has a deficit in its balance of trade (i.e. its imports exceed its exports) there is a resultant excess supply of the country's currency in the international currency market. This would lead to a downward tendency of the currency's rate of exchange under a flexible exchange system. Under a fixed exchange system, the excess currency supply would have to be absorbed by the respective Central Bank, so that the pressure on the rate of exchange is neutralised. In other words, the excess supply would have to be purchased against payment of foreign exchange. This would lead to a depletion of the foreign exchange reserves of the country.

This is, of course, the textbook story – a part of the ideological state apparatus – that contributes to the hegemony[7] of capital. That is, this story (or, more fashionably, narrative) is part of the cultural material that is generated by capital in the course of its genesis and expansion, and which plays its part in convincing the people that the capitalist system is the best.

We have seen that, in reality, the foreign exchange reserves of a country need not decline on account of a deficit in its balance of payments. Up to the beginning of the 1970s, the USA faced no such difficulties, in spite of regular deficits, because the 'free world' had chosen Uncle Sam as its leader. Hence the USA could import against dollar payment. It could spend more than it earned in the international market just as the central government of a country can, domestically, by printing notes. Obviously, the poor countries never have such options. Deficits on their balance of trade became a recurrent affair for these countries for a number of historical reasons, all related to their colonial past.[8] In such cases the IMF and the rich countries put pressure on these countries to devalue[9] their currencies. The argument was that imports would decrease and exports increase as a result of devaluation. The prices of our exports are set in rupees. So, if the foreign exchange price of the rupee is lowered, less foreign exchange will have to be paid per unit of the commodity. Which means that prices of our exports, in terms of foreign currencies should decrease and consequently their attractiveness to foreign buyers should increase, if the domestic currency is devalued. The prices of the commodities we import are set in terms of foreign exchange. Hence, by the converse logic, the prices paid by domestic buyers for these commodities – in terms of rupees – should increase, and their attractiveness should decrease if the domestic currency is devalued. It was, therefore, argued that chronically deficit countries should devalue their currencies, to overcome their deficit.

In reality, it was seen that devaluation did not lead to improvement in the payments situation of these countries, and on the contrary, in most of the cases severely aggravated the problem. One reason suggested for this was the general commodity composition of the imports and exports of these countries. In most cases their exports consisted of necessities, like food. The demand for such commodities rises only marginally if their prices decline. Again, if demand does not rise appreciably as a result of devaluation (to be precise, at a rate greater than the rate of devaluation), foreign exchange earning will actually decline in spite of increase in the quantum of exports. This is because the price of the rupee in terms of foreign exchange is reduced through devaluation. Supply price of our exports are stated in terms of rupees, so on account of devaluation the amount of foreign exchange earned per unit of export falls. The demand for imported commodities may fall on account of the rise in their prices in terms of rupees. To the extent that this occurs, there will be a decline in the foreign exchange payments on account of imports assuming that the supply prices of such commodities (given in terms of foreign exchange) remain unchanged. It must also be borne in mind that machines, spares, and other necessary inputs constitute part of the imports of the poor countries from the rich countries. The demand for such imports is unlikely to be influenced by devaluation. So, in almost all cases devaluation failed as a cure for the balance of payments deficits of poor countries. On the contrary, production costs increased, inflation rate increased (causing further deficit in the balance of payments[10]), and international debts of the country increased.

In the first phase of its operation, apart from fixing exchange rates, the principal task of IMF was to bail out countries with balance of payments difficulties by providing short-term loans from its own fund, which had been built with members' contributions. The Fund did not begin extending credit before 1950. The principal reason was the lack of unanimity between the UK and the USA regarding the terms on which loans were to be extended. The opinion of poor countries was of no consequence as their voting strength was negligible. At that time the UK was of the opinion that IMF should extend unconditional loans to its members to meet their balance of payments deficits. The US position was that IMF should extend loans only on condition that it was given the right to monitor whether, or not, the borrower was undertaking appropriate policies to overcome its balance of payments difficulties. The differences in the economic conditions of the UK and the USA explain the differences in their positions regarding loan conditionality of IMF. One could not imagine a situation where the USA would have to borrow. On the other hand, the UK was the largest borrower during the first twenty years of the functioning of the Fund. Besides, the political stance of the British Labour Party and the political prestige enjoyed, internationally, by the UK at that time also partly explains the intensity of the conflict. Keynesian principles were used to sustain the stand taken by the UK. It was argued that if the principal objective of fiscal and monetary policies was to achieve equilibrium in the balance of payments, then these instruments could not be used to generate domestic demand.[11] This could have disastrous consequences for employment.

Naturally, the American argument was ultimately accepted. It was decided in 1952 that, whether, or not a country's loan application would be accepted would depend entirely on the policies proposed by the applicant to overcome its own balance of payments deficit. It was also decided that the greater the ratio of the amount of loan sought to the country's quota more restrictive would be the loan conditionality. These conditions are part of the stabilisation programme of the IMF and the World Bank. The main objective of this programme is to force governments to reduce their expenditure. Most of the reduction is to be achieved through retrenchment of public sector employees and de-indexation[12] of wages of public sector enterprises.

Initially, the conditions were not clearly spelt out. Almost all nations other than the USA used to believe that governments should have independence in formulating domestic policy. But the USA would veto all loan applications in which the proposed set of policies did not meet with their approval. So, effectively, the stabilisation policy proposed by the USA became the condition for grant of loan, even before it was officially accepted by the IMF.

The Second Phase: Involvement in Domestic Policy Decisions

From the first half of the 1970s, the USA began to lose its sole leadership of the so-called free world. Consequently, it was forced to devalue the dollar on account of the massive deficits in its balance of payments. As long as the dollar was almost the sole medium of international transactions, the US deficit did not pose any problem. As we have discussed, if the currency of a country is accepted as the international medium of payments, it can spend more than it earns, just as the government of a nation can systematically incur deficits in its domestic transaction, simply by printing money (which the citizens are bound to accept). But as other capitalist nations, like Germany, France, and Japan became economically stronger, the dollar lost its pre-eminence. And, faced with massive deficits, the dollar had to be devalued twice in 1970-71. Free convertibility between gold and dollars was also suspended. Because of the fluctuations in the value of the dollar, the fixed exchange rate system that had been in force since Bretton Woods now broke down. Under the fixed exchange system brokered by the IMF, all currency prices were expressed in dollars. Once the standard itself tottered, the system crumbled. The worldwide fixed exchange system ceased to exist; various currency arrangements were established. But the trend was towards floating exchange rates (i.e. exchange rates determined by 'market forces') and full convertibility. The international economic organisations, like the IMF, began pressurising its members to adopt this system.

In this age of globalisation, one constantly hears arguments in favour of leaving the determination of the prices of commodities in the hands of the market. This is a myth produced by capitalist society – the market as subject. The unstated argument is basically to leave the determination of prices in the hands of the powers that control the market. For instance, leaving the determination of exchange rates to the market, in the current context, means leaving their determination to the whims or expectations of the speculators in the currency and short-term capital markets. The writing was on the wall. This was the direction in which exchange rate determination was headed.

The year 1976 was very significant in the history of IMF. That year the UK had to take a massive loan from the IMF to tide over its foreign exchange crisis. The conditions imposed by IMF were such that its intervention in the domestic economy assumed far more extensive proportions than ever before. Reduction in government expenditure, particularly the promise to cut important social welfare expenditures was part of the conditions. Apart from this, curtailing government deficits, prior announcement of the proposed rate of expansion of money supply, relaxation of controls on exports were also insisted upon. The basic idea behind these conditions was revealed in the pronouncement of the US Secretary of the Treasury, William Simon. He claimed that Britain and other deficit countries were violating an internationally acceptable 'code of behaviour'. One of the requirements of such a code was 'responsible behaviour'. What was meant by responsible behaviour was also explained. It meant setting realistic goals for public policy, which included restructuring of social objectives and a shift of resources away from state enterprise towards private enterprise.[13]

Another Dose of Theory

We had remarked that Primitive Capital Accumulation (PCA) is a never-ending process. Dispossessing communities and collectives of their rights is an inseparable part of the history of every stage of capitalism. With changes in the social and legal system to facilitate such dispossession, the structures of communities are transformed and, consequently, the demands of communities also change. The demand to increase public expenditure on education, healthcare and social security is an expression of such changes in community consciousness, and its own perception of its needs. Having been robbed of their traditional rights through the intervention of the state, working for and at the behest of capital, the transformed and distorted communities turn to their destroyer – the capitalist state itself – for succour.

Let us elaborate. Consider a forest-dependent community. Such tribal communities have their own world outlook. They do not make any positive demands on the state. All they 'demand' is that the state should not deprive them of the right to continue their traditional ways of life. Their life and livelihood is heavily dependent on nature, which is treated as the common property of the community. In fact, as we have remarked elsewhere in this book, the notion of property is quite out of place when talking of the holistic relation between a forest-dependent people and the forest. Ecology is a part of their community existence itself. But primitive capital accumulation is directed towards transforming forest resources, natural water supply and such other, into private property. To achieve this, the traditional rights of the tribals have to be abolished. This is achieved through various processes, one of the most important being the construction of large dams, which drive these communities from their hearth and home. Another weapon that is gradually gaining in significance in India is the displacement of agricultural communities for creation of industrial enclaves, housing resorts for the very rich and for realty business. The state is directly expropriating the lands using a colonial Land Acquisition Act. This process is strikingly reminiscent of the enclosure movement that occurred in Britain in the eighteenth century.[14] These displaced people flock to the urban settlements in the hope of securing some means of livelihood. They live as the dregs of urban society. Having lost their traditional community support system, they become entirely dependent on the largesse of the state to eke out an existence. Thus, from a position of fierce independence, they shift to a position where they join the other urban poor in demanding that the state provide healthcare, education and social security.[15]

Arguments in favour of the demands for state funding of education, healthcare and social security are also advanced by academics who subscribe to the virtues of the market, using the language of capital and the categories of the market. It is claimed that services like health and education benefit not only those who directly consume them, but also other members of the society they inhabit. In technical jargon, one would say that enjoyment of healthcare and educational facilities by one individual generates 'external economies' for some others. The community or society in which the individual resides is also benefited. An educated person elects people's representatives wisely. If an infected person is cured of a contagious disease, people around are relieved of the threat of the contagion. But in the market, people only pay for the benefit they directly derive. The individual buyer does not pay for the social benefit. So, if health and education are supplied through the market, their supply will be less than is socially desired because their appropriate price is not paid. This is as far as the formal logic within the bounds of market transactions goes – what one gets in the textbooks, which are part of the ideological state apparatus. Later we will see in what way the idea of social benefit is a part of the ideological state apparatus, that is, in what sense it plays a significant part in dissimulating the fundamental discrimination at the base of the capitalist system. Looked at from the perspective of interest groups, the demand for increasing public expenditure on social welfare schemes is one expression of the self-realisation of the rights of the community of working people, under the given capitalist circumstances. On the one hand, there is the ever-unsatisfied desire of capital to abolish the community rights of the working people through the continuous expansion of the market. On the other hand, there is a desperate attempt by the working people to limit the market, by pressurising the government so that collective rights can be established in new forms. The demand that the state should take the responsibility of providing education, healthcare, potable water, etc. is part of this effort on the part of the working people. The justification for such demands directly conflicts with the market ideology, which does not recognise any social need, that is a need other than the demand, which one can satisfy through purchase in the market. So the demand for increasing government expenditure on these fronts has significance beyond a simple reallocation of expenditure – it signifies the attempt to force the state to accommodate an ethics which conflicts with the ethics of globalisation, with the ethics of the marketplace. It is the ethics born out of the communitarian perception that all members have the right to life – a right that supersedes all other rights.

Understanding the Changes

The significance of the new turn that IMF policies took in 1976 has to be analysed in the context of this continuous process of struggle around PCA. The IMF nearly assumed the role of Supreme Commander in the capitalist war of occupation. That the conditions imposed by the IMF were not justifiable by any stretch of scientific reasoning – on which issue erudite intellectuals write volumes – was quite clear to the formulators of this policy, like William Simon. He says openly, without prevarication, that the issue is one of capitalist ethics, of the capitalist notion of what is just. The labour party government had chalked out a programme of massive social expenditure on the basis of a certain ethics of rights. The IMF forced the government to adopt a completely opposite set of policies on the basis of a different ethics of rights. It is most significant that the first victims of IMF's new, aggressive policies were the working people of a developed capitalist country, and when government authority in that country was in the hands of the Labour Party, at that point of time still vaguely a working people's party. In terms of time, place and target nation, the conditions imposed by IMF had profound symbolic significance. When a professedly leftist government promises unlimited right of entry to foreign capital, this is of much greater import than if the same had been promised by a rightist or even a centrist government. And that the nation was developed made the impact even greater. If the economic sovereignty of a first world nation could be curbed, poor countries would be easy prey. Another significant event of the decade was the oil shock. In 1973 the OPEC countries increased the price of petroleum by seventy per cent, in one shot. All developed countries, other than Britain, had the financial resources to tackle the problem. The poor countries, however, had to borrow large amounts in the capital market. In the beginning, the commercial financial institutions, mainly the commercial banks of developed countries, invested huge amounts in what they saw as new and endless avenues for interest earning. But, soon the banks found themselves in an awkward dilemma, as these countries lacked the ability to pay even the interest on the loans, let alone repay their debts. At this juncture IMF emerged as their saviour.

Up to this point of time, the IMF had lent mainly to the rich countries. Now, in order to bail out the banks, which were unable to recover their loans, most of the loans of the IMF began to be advanced to the poor countries. The IMF had to increase its loanable funds to meet the requirements of the new target group. It first increased its own resources. For this it increased members' quotas. New programmes and projects were initiated for lending to the third world.

Together with shifting its focus to the third world countries, IMF also made its conditions more stringent. From this time on, the IMF and the World Bank began to coordinate their control over countries that sought loans in a more organised manner. The basic philosophy continued to be the one that had been spelt out in 1976 – force such nations to work towards uncontrolled markets (what it really meant was that these organisations were now committed to freeing the markets from any constraint that governments of poor countries may impose), markets over which the governments of the small countries did not have any control. The necessary policy changes were grouped into short-term and long-term policy requirements. The policies that these nations were required to adopt in the short term were contained in what was called the Stabilisation Programme.[16] The long-term policies were spelt out in the Structural Adjustment Programme.[17] Since the early 1980s, the IMF was entrusted with the task of enforcing the Stabilisation Programme, while the World Bank was assigned the job of forcing the Structural Adjustment Programme on the debtor nations. (Peet, Richard, 2003, p.121). The IMF reinvented itself as almost an underwriter[18] for the private financial institutions, extending loans to the poor countries on condition that these agencies lent against IMF certification only.

Current Phase: the Demise of Sovereignty

The policies that the IMF currently pursues were initiated during the 1970s through the conditions imposed on the UK. James Baker, the US Treasury secretary from 1985 to 1988, gave them their final shape. His plan is known as the 'Baker Plan'. Mexico and Brazil faced a grave financial crisis at the beginning of the 1980s. Free market economists had been touting these as model economies. But, the attempt to generate growth with free international trade led to huge deficits in the balance of trade of these countries. Initially, these deficits were met with inflow of foreign capital. The deficit in the trade account was covered by commercial loans, direct foreign investment and inflow of speculative capital. But, soon this apparent balance collapsed under the weight of its internal contradictions. Since the deficit in the balance of trade was not diminishing, the inflow of foreign capital had to keep increasing every year in order to meet the interest and loan repayment liabilities of the two countries. Once the foreign investors realised that there was no foreseeable possibility of these nations escaping from the debt trap, they began decreasing their investments in these countries. A crisis developed, which was heightened by the sudden outflow of speculative capital.[19] The Baker Plan was drawn up to deal with the situation.

The Baker Plan was a plan to bail out creditor nations and institutions from the imminent threat of default by debtor countries. In a sense it was just giving formal shape to what had already been happening since the beginning of the 1980s. It was envisaged that the World Bank and the IMF should work jointly to ensure that the lenders did not have to write off their loans to such permanently indebted countries, because of the inability of these countries to service their debts.[20] These two international agencies should increase their loans to countries, such as Mexico and Brazil, and should also influence commercial banks to do the same. But these loans had to be made conditional on the borrower nations' accepting the Stabilisation Programme and the Structural Adjustment Programme, the first being administered by the IMF and the second by the World Bank. The plan also calculated in detail the amount of loans that had to be advanced by the World Bank, the IMF and the commercial banks, respectively.[21]

It is unnecessary to explain the significance of each programme separately. In essence, the programme is the same as that contained in the conditions imposed on Britain when it took the loan in 1976 – to ensure the conditions which can allow capital to occupy all territories; use the economic powers of the state to uproot all attempts to define and establish new collective or community rights.

Protest – Resistance

As long as the IMF had not intervened in domestic policy, the debate about IMF policies was restricted to the arena of conflict between nations. The attitude of a government towards IMF policies depends on the relative strengths of the interest groups within the nation. At the crucial juncture in the mid-1970s, the Labour Party, which still largely had a working-class ethos, was in power in Britain. So the conflict between the working people's response to IMF policies and the response of big capital to the policies was played out as the conflict between the UK and the USA.

When the IMF began to impose harsh conditions on the domestic sector, resistance began to spread to the third world. In the beginning it took the form of spontaneous food riots. The marketable economists tried to explain away all the economic devastation caused by these policies as a passing phenomenon. They claimed that that there was no reason to worry about the alarming increase in unemployment, caused by cut-back of government expenditure and the sudden demise of domestic enterprises under pressure of unbridled imports. That there was even no need to be concerned about the sharp rise in the prices of food. That a bright future was just round the corner. The starved naturally showed much less patience than these well-heeled intellectuals. So the riots started. Later the protests took more organised shape.

People protested against the economic policies that they perceived to be causing their ruin. They protested against wage cuts. They protested against lay-offs and decrease in government subsidies. Through the 1970s and 1980s food riots, partial and general strikes, which sometimes extended for weeks and even months, broke out in Argentina, Egypt, Morocco, the Dominican Republic, Venezuela, Indonesia, and in other parts of the globe. The governments met these protests with severe brutality. Twenty people were killed in army firing in Egypt. According to the Socialist Movement, six hundred and thirty-seven people lost their lives in Morocco, the majority of whom were women and children. Fifty people were killed and four thousand injured in the Dominican Republic. From the end of the 1980s these protests began to be internationally organised. This form of protest was initiated at the venue of the IMF's annual meeting in 1988. More than twenty thousand people marched in protest in Berlin, the venue of the meeting. Significantly, none of the people who joined the march had come from poor countries. They were members of various leftist organisations in the Western countries.

The distorted globalisation of today is leading to globalisation of capitalist occupation. All nations are being forced to adopt a uniform set of laws and economic policies to facilitate capital's expansionism. What is heartening is that this homogenisation is also sparking the first global kinship of the working people. When capital goes global, conditions become more appropriate for labour to go global. It is, of course, not an automatic corollary. Both the nationally powerful classes and interest groups as well as entrenched trade unions and the ruling left, preach the importance of nations and nationalism even more stridently. The working people also fall prey to the motivated propaganda that the presence of 'aliens', within the country, is the root cause of all their misfortunes. They are told that if these religious and ethnic 'outsiders' could be driven out, then there would be sufficient jobs for all. Communal and ethnic violence follow. Yet one can see a ray of hope when the people of the first world join in their thousands, to protest against the sufferance of the poor in the third world, caused by globalisation.

NOTES

1. Lenin, who was the most important leader of the socialist revolution in Russia, had proposed that after the revolution (which established the rule of the working class) there would be a period of transition to the next stage – the stage of Communism. When communism, the highest stage of social evolution, was established, society would cease to be divided into classes. So the state, as the organisation of class rule would wither away in this process of transition. (Lenin, V.I., 1992)
2. As we go along, it will become clear why we are using this epithet. Feudal plunder is appropriation of rent through politically created titles on resources, which are intrinsically immobile, like land, or which are rendered immobile through definite policy, like knowledge in the present era. In contrast, capitalist plunder consists of the appropriation of profit through the working of the apparently impersonal market, which is a place of mutual exchange of titles of equal 'value'. For such exchange to be possible, it is necessary that there should not be any extra economic (say, political) constraint on the possession or transfer of such titles. It is our contention, however, that capitalist plunder is inevitably intertwined with feudal plunder.
3. Such societies, which are arguably the earliest form in which humans organised themselves, have been characterised as classless. Class division, that is the division into the surplus producers and the surplus appropriators, can occur only when society produces a surplus over and above its subsistence requirements. In other words surplus production is a necessary condition for the existence of class divisions. Since science and technology were (are) very rudimentary in these societies, such

societies did not (or do not) produce any surplus. Hence class divisions do not exist.

4. My local context compels me to elaborate on the nature of collaboration involved on the part of this particular state government. The Tatas, a prominent industrial house in India, had reached an agreement with the leftist government in West Bengal, to set up a car-manufacturing unit at a place called Singur. The land earmarked for the project is very fertile and produces multiple crops. Converting multiple-crop land to non-agricultural land violates the state government's own announced policy, but that is a separate issue. The farmers are, by and large, vehemently opposed to the government's plan to acquire their lands for handing over to the Tatas. (We are writing in the present tense because the government is perpetrating the atrocity even as we write.) A major opinion, which comes through in the interviews given by the farmers is that all the talk of compensation – even if one were to ignore the failure to keep the promises made previously by the state government in similar cases – is quite meaningless to these peasants. What is the correct quantum of compensation? They lead a life that quite satisfies their physical and cultural demands. For this they are totally dependent on their plots of land. It is as much a part of their culture and life, as it is a means of livelihood. The peasants have a holistic culture that directly opposes the commodity culture of globalisation. The concept of land as commodity is thoroughly alien to their culture. From our cultural perspective, which refuses any holistic or ecological position, we can invent a justification of their stand: loss of land will deprive the peasants of the opportunity to work, even if they can earn sufficient interest income from the monetary compensation without doing any work! Of course, the state government is using violence to intimidate the organisation formed by the peasants, to resist the attempts of the government to evict them from their land. But the 'left' parties in power have also asked their mass organisations to 'explain' to the peasants that the money being offered is more than sufficient compensation. In other words, these organisations are being deployed to carry out the task of cultural transformation – from a holistic culture to the commodity culture that is consistent with the needs of global capital. This experience also teaches another important lesson – the significance of an over-deterministic or interdependent approach. It is not just a question of economic transformation

that is involved, but changes at all levels of social existence and perception. (See Basu, P. K., 2007)

5. '...but the accumulation of capital presupposes surplus-value; surplus-value presupposes capitalist production; capitalist production presupposes the pre-existence of considerable masses of capital and of labour-power in the hands of producers of commodities. The whole movement, therefore, seems to turn in a vicious circle, out of which we can only get by supposing *a primitive accumulation (previous accumulation of Adam Smith) preceding capitalist accumulation; an accumulation not the result of the capitalist mode of production, but its starting point.'* (Marx, K., 1954, p. 667. Italics added.)
6. We have already introduced this type of capital. Here we are talking of a specific kind of speculative capital: speculative capital invested in currency speculation. Such speculators invest capital to buy up those currencies whose price, in terms of other currencies, they think will rise. Simultaneously, they sell those currencies whose price they expect to fall. If their speculations about the changes in exchange rates turn out to be correct, then they make huge gains by selling at enhanced prices, the currencies they had purchased.
7. All dominating segments and classes maintain their control over the dominated or subordinated segments and classes through both coercion and persuasion. The means of persuasion are various. They include religion, popular culture, education, theories of social being and change, etc. These are not all, or even largely, consciously or conspiratorially generated. They, as much the products of the system, are significant constituents of the social order. These instruments of persuasion generate acceptance of the current social hierarchy in the psyche of the dominated. At this point, the dominating segments would be said to have achieved *hegemony*. In the process of generation of hegemony, there are some adaptive changes in the dominant segments way of thinking and the manner of surplus extraction. The subordinated segments too adapt. To mark this process of adaptive change in securing hegemony, some have preferred the term '*synthetic hegemony*' (Chaudhury, A., 1994, Chaudhury A., et al., 2000). We have already introduced the reader to this term in our introductory chapter.
8. The colonial economies were each distorted in specific ways by the imperial powers, depending on the natural resources and the type of economy that existed when the imperial country

occupied the colony. But, there were certain patterns in the distortions of the colonial economies by the imperial countries. India, for example, was transformed from an exporter of industrial wares to an importer of such commodities. Its land settlement was distorted in a manner that would allow the British to maximise their land revenue. A class of parasitic moneylenders was promoted to provide finance to the peasants to pay their rent dues, out of which the revenue demands of the government were met. Both these factors contributed to the low productivity of the agricultural sector. This structure was inherited by post-colonial India. So there was little that the country could export at the time of independence. So, post-colonial India suffered from chronic balance of payments deficits. The same story was repeated, with local variations, for each colony.

9. See note 5 p. 33.
10. If the rate of inflation in our country exceeds that in a country with which we trade, then the price of our import competing goods will rise faster than that of the import goods. So the import competing goods will gradually lose their markets. Conversely, inflation causes the prices of the goods that are exported from our country to rise faster than the prices of the competing goods produced in the importing countries. As a result, demand for the goods exported from our country declines.
11. For example, if unemployment exists, then Keynesian principles suggest that the government should increase its spending to increase the demand for domestic manufactures. But this policy causes increase in National Income (NI) and so leads to rise in consumer demand, which includes the demand for imported consumer goods. This will lead to a deterioration of the balance of trade of the country. So, if trade balance is the primary objective, then the government cannot be free to spend in order to generate domestic demand.
12. A part of the wages and salaries of most employees of the organised sector, and especially of the public sector, used to be linked to the price index. This facility is still enjoyed by a large part of the traditional organised sector, though this is denied to the new labour force in the sunrise industries. This part is called the 'dearness allowance'. If such allowance is paid, then as prices of commodities increase there is some automatic increase in the wages and salaries. This, partially, compensates the employees for the reduction in their ability to purchase goods and services caused by the increase in the prices. The ethics behind the

Stabilisation Programme totally ignores the question of social justice involved in the payments to employees. It is, therefore, blind to the need for compensating them for the loss in purchasing power caused by inflation. It subscribes to the faith that whatever is earned through bargaining in the market is justified. If some employees lose out on account of inflation, and do not have the ability to renegotiate their contract, then they deserve to lose. The only aspect of indexed wages that bothers these stabilisers is that it reinforces inflationary pressure. When price is raised, profit increases. If wages are indexed, wages rise in consequence. This lowers profits. So the capitalists increase prices further. And so on. Obviously, one way out of this is to de-index wages. If profit is to be left untouched, this is the only option available.

13. Peet, Richard, 2003: 70.
14. As we go along, it will become clear why we are using this epithet. Feudal plunder is appropriation of rent through politically created titles on resources, which are intrinsically immobile, like land, or which are rendered immobile through definite policy, like knowledge in the present era. In contrast, capitalist plunder consists of the appropriation of profit through the working of the apparently impersonal market, which is a place of mutual exchange of titles of equal 'value'. For such exchange to be possible, it is necessary that there should not be any extra economic (say, political) constraint on the possession or transfer of such titles. It is our contention, however, that capitalist plunder is inevitably intertwined with feudal plunder.
15. Of course, this is not a static attitude either. They perceive, at some point of time, that they cannot sustain themselves within the legal system of the market economy. This realisation is accelerated as the state begins to be motivated, more and more, by the ethics of the market alone. Concerns of social justice, health and education for all become increasingly unjustifiable to the dominant ideology. Justice is what the market decides. The displaced tribals are forced to live a life that brands them as anti-socials, according to the ruling ethics and legality. Their relations to the state, to the party in power, and their demands from these institutions now undergo another metamorphosis. They cannot afford to live in legal residences, so they build illegal shanties, which the powers that be tolerate because of political exigencies. Forced out of legal means of livelihood, they often resort to various illegal means of earning a living, like smuggling,

peddling drugs, etc. But that is another story, which we will narrate later.

16. The key components of the 'Stabilisation Programme' included: devaluation of currency; curtailment of government expenditure through reduction in the number of public sector employees and drastic cuts in social sector spending; market liberalisation (i.e. elimination of subsidies, price controls, curbs on entry); de-indexation of wages (see footnote 10).
17. The Structural Adjustment Programme included: liberalisation of trade; liberalisation of the banking sector, including the privatisation of state-owned financial sector; withdrawal of the state from social sector programmes like education and healthcare, and privatisation of these programmes on the basis of the cost recovery principle; reorganisation of the state sector in order to eliminate 'unproductive' expenditures (basically meaning the retrenchment of state sector employees); tax reforms to reduce the burden of taxes on the segment that invests (i.e. the rich).
18. An organisation that guarantees loans advanced by another organisation is called an underwriter. In other words, the underwriter gives a pledge to the lending agency that it would repay the loan in case of default by the borrower.
19. We have already noted that speculative capital is more volatile than productive capital (footnote 5 of chapter 2). At the first hint of some economic crisis, it is this component of capital that leaves the country, further heightening the crisis. In fact, it was felt by many commentators that the crisis that Mexico faced – with regard to the financial distress caused by the sudden flight of speculative capital, particularly portfolio investment – was most likely to be repeated elsewhere. Hence, this phenomenon was named the Mexico Syndrome.
20. Debt servicing means the payment of interest and repayment of principal amount of loan.
21. Accustomed as we are to thinking in a market-oriented way, a certain doubt may creep into our mind at this point: if these policies were really capable of ensuring their objectives, should they not have been beneficial to the borrower countries also? After all, I must be economically better off if I am able to repay my debts than if I am not able to repay them. What is true for an individual is not applicable to the aggregate. In general, within any aggregate where economic inequality is rampant, further concentration and intensification of inequality is a precondition

for increment in the ability of the aggregate to service debts or to make any obligatory payment outside the aggregate, like a tribute, say. It is only the rich segments that have the wherewithal to save. Hence, if their share in the total income increases, savings of the aggregate will increase, and so will its capacity to repay loans, pay interest or pay any form of tribute. An interesting corroboration of this can be found in the colonial history of India. One of the reasons for the replacement of the traditional overflow system of irrigation with the canal system was the need to concentrate the gains of productivity over a small region. This made both the collection and land revenues easier.

4

The World Bank: The Humane Mask

Preliminaries

There is no difference in the structures of administration and governance of the IMF and the World Bank, so we will not discuss these aspects separately. We will just remind the reader that the structures of administration and governance of both organisations are similar to those of a commercial bank. This similarity has a deep significance. Neither IMF nor the World Bank can violate the limits set by the accounting rules and procedures of a capitalist financial organisation.

The World Bank has four arms:

The International Bank for Reconstruction and Development, IBRD. Formalised at the Bretton Woods Conference, it started functioning in 1946. IBRD gives loans to individual countries for 'development' projects, guarantees loans and provides consultancy services for evaluation of loan prospects. IBRD acquires finances from the international finance market. From this stock it lends at near-market rates of interest for the projects it approves.

The International Development Association, IDA. Established in 1960, it extends development loans to the poorest of the poor nations that are not considered loan-worthy by the capital market. It lends out of the funds generated by members' contributions. The borrower does not have to pay any interest, though an administrative charge is levied at a low rate.

The International Finance Corporation, IFC. Established in 1959, it is the greatest multilateral source of credit and share capital for private sector investment in underdeveloped countries.

Multilateral Investment Guarantee Agency, MIGA. Established in 1988, it ensures private foreign capital against risks like civil wart, nationalisation, etc.

Additionally, the **International Centre for Settlement of Investment Disputes**, ICSID, was established under the World Bank for settlement of disputes between the host country governments and foreign investors.

According to the Bretton Woods agreement, the World Bank was established for some specific purposes. Major among these were:

(*i*) Reconstruction of war-devastated economies and for encouraging the utilisation of resources in the borrower countries.

(*ii*) Encouraging foreign investment through guarantees (of repayment) of loans extended internationally by private agencies. It was also expected to encourage such flow by demonstrating its confidence in enterprises, through equity participation[1] in such ventures.

(*iii*) Encouraging foreign investment in order to induce the growth of international trade with long-term stability.

(*iv*) Arranging the loans that it advances or guarantees in such a way as to ensure that the more useful or more urgently required projects are executed on a priority basis.

Commercial Banker

It is not possible to determine the basic objective of the World Bank from the long list of intentions (which we have already whittled down to basics). Arguably, the lack of clarity at its very inception is reflective of the need to evade conflicts of interests. In practice, as the ruling orthodoxy has evolved in the USA, and changed its position from time to time, so the policies of the World Bank have also undergone changes. Because of the overly broad and unclear objectives of the Bank, it has been possible to maintain consistency between the changing policies and the professed objectives.

As in the case of the IMF, the USA has complete control over the Bank's policies because the Bank mainly depends on US capital, both official and private. The USA can block any major change in the Bank's Charter as this requires 85 per cent of the votes and USA alone owns 16.4 per cent of the votes. With the exception of two, all the Presidents of the Bank were earlier employed by commercial banks or investment banks or were lawyers whose major clients were such banks. All of them were citizens of the USA. Though its Articles of Association do not specify the nationality of the institution's president, by a long-standing convention, the Bank's president is a US national while the managing director of the International Monetary Fund, the Bank's sister organisation, is European. Robert Zoellick became the eleventh president of the World Bank on July 1, 2007. Robert Zoellick is former Deputy Secretary of the US State Department and the former Chairman of Goldman Sachs' Board of International Advisors.

Initially, under the influence of orthodox commercial banking ideas, the World Bank based its fiscal and monetary policy prescriptions on the need to balance income and expenditure. Hence, it was required that even in the short run, borrowers would have to balance their international transactions account. To ensure this, the Bank only extended loans for specific projects. The Bank mainly advanced loans for infrastructural projects, like electricity generation and transport, because such projects can be directly monitored and the profit or loss can be easily accounted for and ascertained using market principles. So the Bank could predict the possibility of interest payment and loan repayment with some degree of certainty. The Bank was not interested in programme lending. For instance, it was not interested in providing loans for planned extension of educational or health network. In this phase the Bank's activities were limited to reconstruction of Second World War-devastated countries. One can safely comment that the Bank's thinking was strictly in line with the unyielding strand of an individualistic culture. There was not even a hint of bourgeois humanism or liberal bourgeois thought.

The humane face of the Bank

From the mid-1950s the rich countries began to feel concerned about the lack of development of the poor countries. There were many reasons for this sympathy, among which bourgeois liberalism was undoubtedly important. But the need to compete with socialist countries as friends of the poor was, perhaps, of overriding concern to the ruling segments at that juncture. The US Secretary of State, John Foster Dulles, had commented, 'it may be good banking to put South America through the wringer, but it will come out red'. So, it turns out that, what often appears as humanism, might be nothing more than sound market logic, seen from a long-run perspective. Too much economic pressure might irreparably damage the political commitment of the borrower country to run the economy according to market principles. And this would be to the detriment of the interests of the Bank and also to global capital as a whole.

The very concept of economic development changed as the influence of rigid individualism, or at least its open propaganda, began to wane. Focus shifted from investment in infrastructure for increasing productivity, to welfare schemes for reducing poverty. From this time on, one could glimpse the 'humane face' of the Bank. We need to understand what humanism means in this particular context, because unlike, say, the concept of 'profit' there is no uncontested definition of human values.

'Humanism' does not have any fixed meaning that the term evokes across all societies and at all times. It may, generally, be interpreted as a desire to help those who do not have the power to help themselves. This involves more than a touch of paternalism. It generally also requires marginal empowerment of those who lack power. 'Marginal' because such empowerment is not intended to overthrow the existing power to extract surplus produced by the labouring people. Of course, any empowerment, which is not directly the result of the working of the system itself, disturbs the system. Pushed to the limit, it has always the potential of dislodging the existing power structure. For example, caste discrimination may not have been a necessary component of the feudal power of the *zamindar* to extract rent. So, empowerment of the outcastes could have been a valid humanitarian project during the *zamindari* period. But this empowerment, itself, could have partly eroded the power of the *zamindar*, as he would invariably belong to the upper castes. Besides, a movement for social empowerment is likely to lead to a movement for economic power.

In a country that has a non-capitalist socio-economic structure, qualitative differences in rights are accepted. For example, the upper castes had the right to work less and appropriate more of what was produced. (As a matter of fact, they still enjoy that privilege, but that is now by dint of property rights over greater amount of resources). In this situation, empowerment of the outcastes would require a change in the qualitative structure of rights. But in a capitalist society, apparently (that is, seen from the uncritical perspective of the market, which has become ingrained in us) there is no qualitative inequality, no hierarchy. If one has money one can acquire property rights, one can buy and sell (that is, all have the right to enter into exchange contracts). Seen from this angle, the index of lack of power in this society is quantitative. One who does not have money cannot acquire rights. Superficially, one is underprivileged not because one belongs to a lower rung of the social hierarchy, but simply because one does not have a sufficiently large quantity of money. So, the new economics of development tries to reduce quantitative inequality. Development theory[2] cannot conceive of the inequality of rights that is created and maintained by state power, through the process of primitive capital accumulation, because its vision is restricted to the field of market transactions. It is a superficial view. And, like all uncritical ways of looking at society, it does not theoretically challenge the existing order. From our critical perspective, however, we have seen that the apparently impersonal and non-discriminatory market is built on the foundation of a violent dispossession of traditional rights, through the process of primitive capital accumulation. The state, therefore, abets and actively initiates a process of economic discrimination. And this is a never-ending process. On this base of qualitative differentiation, is built the edifice of the market that, on the surface, appears to depend purely on non-discriminatory, or qualitatively equal, rights. But, development economics cannot see all this. Or will not see because it, too, has vested interests. So, the Bank's humanism was restricted to some effort to reduce quantitative inequality, by promoting projects that could lead to a limited amount of redistribution. The attempt to reduce economic inequality increased the scope of the World Bank's activities. It also changed the focus of the Bank: from developed countries to poor countries, and from project loans for infrastructure development to agricultural loans.

In tune with these changes, the IDA (International Development Agency) was created in 1960. From the early 1960s the poorness of a country, defined by its per-capita income replaced its loan servicing ability as the index of eligibility for Bank loans. After some experimentation, the Integrated Rural Development Project was inaugurated. Under this programme the World Bank was to aid small farmers within a defined geographical area to increase productivity and marketable surplus. It was decided that the Bank would extend financial assistance for providing the major agricultural inputs (seeds, fertilisers) and for constructing the necessary infrastructure for agricultural development. Apart from this, the Bank would provide technological consultancy services. These liberal policies were adopted during the tenure of McNamara, President of the World Bank from 1968 to 1981. But towards the end of his term, the Bank's own Operation Evaluation Department expressed the opinion that these programmes had not been successful. The major reason for this failure, according to the evaluation, was lack of land reforms. As a result, the medium and rich farmers were appropriating the benefits that were supposed to accrue to the poor farmers. Inequality was, in fact, increasing instead of declining.

Back to Commercial Norms

From the middle of the 1980s, the World Bank went back to the policy of deciding loan eligibility and choice of projects to be aided on the basis of commercial criteria. The Baker Plan[3] was initiated in the middle of the 1980s. After this the Bank resumed extension of massive loans to the poor countries. But now the declared conditions for extending such loans included liberalisation, privatisation, and curtailment of government expenditure. A country would be given loans only if its government accepted these conditions. In this phase there was virtually no difference between the policies of the World Bank and the IMF. Only if a poor country sacrificed its economic sovereignty and accepted policies favourable to globalised capital, would it be given financial assistance by these institutions.

Some feel that the balance of World Bank's policies have again begun to shift since the second half of the 1990s. In 1998, the President of the World Bank announced a Comprehensive Development Framework (CDF). The fiscal and monetary policies contained in this CDF are extremely conservative. But, at the same time, the CDF also stresses the importance of honest administration, the need for strengthening individual liberties and property rights, and human development measured in terms of criteria like healthcare and education.

Not all agree with this reading of the implications of the policy changes initiated since the second half of the 1990s. Some think that the changes are only cosmetic. Our position is that in general, the core of the Bank's policies must remain conservative, favouring capitalist modernising. The social welfare policies of the Bank must ultimately be severely constrained by this vision. The arguments advanced in favour of this critical assessment of the Bank's supposed change of heart are the same as those that are advanced to critique the social welfare policies of the World Bank in general. Let us examine them.

Policy Contradictions: A Lot of theory

Though in certain phases the Bank has emphasised the need for social welfare programmes, it has never retreated from its commitment towards liberalisaton, privatisation, and conservative fiscal policies. The Structural Adjustment Programme and the Stabilisation Programme were erected on the basis of this faith. Later, these programmes were integrated into the Baker Plan, which we have discussed in detail in the previous chapter. The basic contention of conservative fiscal policy is that the government has to maintain a balance between its income and expenditure. Accompanying policies of liberalisation and privatisation are meant to encourage private enterprise. To this end, the World Bank also exerts influence on debtor countries to reduce tax rates on profit earned by private enterprise. In any case, the per-capita incomes of debtor countries are low. Coupled with this, they also have to reduce the incidence of taxes on the rich. So the revenue earnings of the governments are bound to go down. To maintain the balance between income and expenditure, expenditure has to be reduced. Soft areas[4] are targeted for expenditure reduction. Education, healthcare, water supply – areas that were previously the preserve of the governments – are opened to private enterprise. Foreign competition increases as a result of liberalisation. Domestic production declines in the face of unequal competition. So the propagation of liberalisation, privatisation and conservative fiscal policies conflicts with the Bank's professed concern for social welfare programmes.

But we had stated in the previous chapter that arguments in favour of government expenditure on social welfare are advanced even within neoclassical theory (which builds on the concept of self-sufficient individual), on the basis of the concept of social benefit, which is used to fill up breaches in the logic of individual or private benefit. To repeat a point already made, some tangible goods and intangible services are such that, if they are available to some individuals, others also gain. Provision of healthcare to the poor, for example, generates positive benefits for the rich also, because it reduces the threat of contagion for the latter. This is called external economy or benefit. So the worth to society, of providing healthcare facilities is more than its worth to the individual who directly avails of it. The individual, however, would be willing to pay only for the benefit enjoyed personally. So, the neoclassical theory argues that there is such a thing as social utility, which, in such cases, outstrips the sum of the individual utilities of those who buy these commodities. In such cases public authority should either subsidise the producer for the additional social benefit or should itself take on the responsibility of providing these goods and services. Failing this, these would be under produced because the producer gets paid less than what is its social value. So, the neoclassical theory itself provides a justification for certain types of welfare spending by the government. At the same time, it argues for financial conservatism. How does one explain this phenomenon – the same theory proposing two conflicting policies?

Logically, there should not be any space for community or social being within a discursive space that has the concept of pure, self-centred consciousness as its elementary building block. Therefore, 'social benefit' (which is something more than the aggregation of individual benefits) should not be visible within this discursive scheme. As an example, one may say that it is not possible to conceive contagion within a 'purely' individualistic culture. The culture of the market constantly tells us that it is imperative that we think of self, and self alone. And then the glorious invisible hand of the market will ensure that what is achieved is the best for all. In fact, the individual who thinks of any (person or thing) other than self is branded 'irrational'[5]. But, how would you conceive contagion? Perhaps unexplored territories are waiting to be opened up in medical science, and in philosophy! But, for the time being, one cannot think of 'self-infected' diseases. So it is not possible to argue that government expenditure on healthcare increases benefits to society within a scheme, which conceives of society merely as a summation of self-sufficient individuals. In point of fact, community or society is not just an agglomeration of individuals who are related to one another only through voluntary exchange in the market. Contagion is a relation, which is independent of individual choice. If medical science was trapped within this queer, that is individualistic, notion of society, the concept of contagion could not be articulated. Then how was it possible to think of 'social benefit', of 'externality' within neoclassical theory? In fact, within every theoretical site (for example neoclassical economic theory) theorists often see through 'common sense'. Common sense[6] is a fluid perspective that is based on conceptions, which are derived from disparate theoretical fields, cultures and forces that constitute our thought. That the state has the responsibility to provide for education and healthcare was not argued from a self-centred, bourgeois perspective. Though this was long accepted as a fundamental obligation of the state in a capitalist state, it was possibly the outcome of a paternalistic view of the state that was more appropriate to the feudal system. Even after the demise of the feudal system, the state continued to carry out this obligation, and in a much more liberal and organised manner, because it was deemed necessary from a common sense point of view. The neoclassical theorist sees social benefit through the prism of common sense, a component of which is community consciousness. And because, like all theoretical structures, the neoclassical theory lacks sufficiency, the concept of social utility can be proposed as a supplement[7] to individual utility, to fill up an insufficiency.

This requires some elaboration. The neoclassical theory is based on the single elementary concept of the self-sufficient individual. The only relation that these individuals are permitted is through exchange in the market. But the theorist perceives through common sense that individuals affect one another's well-being and choice directly. They realise that the space of interpersonal relations not mediated by, or formed through the working of, the market cannot be theorised within the neoclassical conceptual world. But, because these relations exist, they influence individual welfare. One realises that there is a yawning gap in the field of vision of neoclassical theory. That is, there is a large area which exists but which cannot be accounted for by this theory. In order to fill up this gap, it generates an entirely new theoretical field of vision through the concept of 'externality' and the related concept of 'social utility'.

These concepts, of course, point to a limitation of self-centred neoclassical theory. But the relation between the two concepts – utility derived by the self-centred individual and social utility

– is not necessarily antagonistic. Thus, in spite of the inconsistencies involved, neoclassical theory peddles two sets of policies, one founded on individual benefits, and the other on social benefits. This also explains the acceptability of development economics to the powers that be.

One needs to understand why the contradiction between the two sets of ideas is non-antagonistic. The bourgeois class is the patron, the bearer of individualism. Its interest inheres in individualism. But no specific class interest is inherent in the notion of an unspecific, ahistorical community in which is rooted the notion of social benefit. That is why there is no inherent antagonism between self-centred neoclassical theory and a development economics that seeks social welfare for an unspecified community or collective. Of course, there is inconsistency between the accounts of commodity exchange based on specific ownership and of social welfare expenditure that is undertaken without any recompensation, or counter-flow of goods or services to the government. Commodity exchange causes commodities of equal value to flow in both directions between the two exchanging parties. Social welfare expenditure by the government does not generate any income for the government in the current period or in the future either. That is why one cannot dovetail the policy of increasing social welfare expenditure with the policy of maintaining balance between the income and expenditure of the government.

Because the idea of social need is not developed from any specific point of view, it is ill defined. It does not bear the stamp of any particular class or group. But the stability of the economic system based on bourgeois individualism can be disturbed by defining social needs in specific ways in particular historical circumstances. So the rule of global capital can be destabilised by organising movements in favour of specific social welfare expenditures. For instance, if there is effective mobilisation around such slogans as 'peace not war', 'reduce expenditure on war, increase expenditure on education and healthcare,' the fraction of capital engaged in manufacturing war commodities, which is a significant segment of global capital, can be seriously hurt.

Under normal circumstances, the ideology of rigid individualism and the welfarist ideology complement each other to generate the cultural dominance of the capitalist order. There is no obvious conflict. In the next chapter we will discuss this issue in much greater detail. Suffice to conclude this chapter with the observation that the World Bank's policies have been guided by both kinds of ideologies, sometimes one and sometimes the other dominating.

NOTES

1. Equity participation in (i.e. purchase of equity or ordinary shares of) a company indicates the confidence of the buyer in the company because in case the venture does not succeed, the equity investor will lose the funds invested in the purchase of the shares.
2. This field is vast and full of diverse potential. It would be supercilious to claim that our comments on the roots and scope of development economics constitute a comprehensive critique of this field of study. But it is, none the less, a serious attempt to look at these issues from a particular perspective – a perspective that we have defined. Implicitly, it is also a reminder of the need for philosophical evaluation of development economics. Our views on these issues are more clearly and rigorously argued in Chapter 4.
3. See page 52-53.
4. Expenditure reduction, expenditure switching from one head to another, increase in taxes, etc. all elicit different reactions in different segments of the population, depending on the differential impact of the particular policy on the respective segment. Some policies might generate less resentment from a particular group, though it causes the same material damage as another policy, simply because its impact is not obvious. For example, wage freeze policy might have the same negative impact on the standard of life of the wage-earning segment of the population, as say, reduction in public healthcare facilities or free educational facilities. But the former policy is likely to generate greater resentment than the latter kind of policies, because the impact of the former is more directly observable. Policies of expenditure reduction or revenue increase that are likely to generate less resentment are 'soft targets' for implementing stabilisation policies.

   Political calculations also determine whether a policy change is a soft target. These cannot be decided a priori, but depend on the current situation. For reasons that we will elaborate on in the concluding chapter of our discussion, the Indian state was more sensitive at the time of independence than it is now, to the demands of the poorer sections for welfare expenditure by the state. So reduction of expenditure on healthcare, education, water supply is much softer targets today than they were in the 1950s and 1960s.

5. In an important part of neoclassical economic theory, which is called 'consumer behaviour' theory, a 'rational consumer' is defined as one whose only objective is to maximise own satisfaction under given circumstances.
6. This footnote is rather tricky and may be skipped for those wanting to get on with it. We are into a difficult terrain – the question of accommodation of reality into the discourse or mode of discussion of a particular discipline or a way of looking at the world. There is a position that was first clearly articulated by a linguist called Saussure (Sturrock, J., 2002), who states that all our thought is constituted by linguistic signs. That is, we think in words, sentences and so on. Reality – what Saussure called the referential world – is never present 'as such' in our thoughts. We represent objects, for example, through common nouns. These are abstractions that represent groups, not a particular object.

   But there are other linguistic views. Particularly important as counter position is the opinion of Charles Pierce. In his view, different symbolic systems can be arranged in order of their ability to access reality. For example, onomatopoeic words resemble what they represent more directly than the letter 'A' standing for a country in international trade theory. The point that Saussure made about the inability of representation systems to access reality is particularly true of the ruling orthodoxy in economics, neoclassical economics, because of its pretension to think within well-defined logical structures, generally models.

   But then, does reality not infringe upon such structures of thought within neoclassical economics, for example, in any way? This is a question that has been explored in great detail by psychoanalysts, like Lacan, (Ross, Stephen, net) who used and developed Saussure's insights. According to Lacan, the real does not enter in any articulate way into our thought, conscious or unconscious. But its presence somewhere acts as a force that is continuously intertwining with other forces, or force fields, to create, among other structures in our mind, conscious thought.

These other force fields include symbolic orders. And the symbolic order tries to contain the disturbance caused by the force of reality by continuously expanding to create surrogates of reality within its own symbolic space. This is how the emergence of the concept of social benefit may be interpreted. We are using a sleight of hand and encapsulating this process in the word-concept 'common sense'. But we have also used this in a broader sense: the thought process of a subject – even a neoclassical economist! – is not completely circumscribed by a single symbolic order. Indeed this is not possible because no order is purely rational and, therefore, there are holes in the symbolic order through which sights seen from other theoretical perspectives intrude. We refer to this process also through the word-concept 'common sense'.

7. This is a common tool used by post-modern thinkers to show the inevitable cracks in the logical surface of argumentation. Because of the unavoidably symbolic nature of all discourse, it is unable to articulate our flux of ideas completely. So,we always have to go on adding and, in the process, amending the previous meaning. One says, for example, that so and so *is* beautiful. Then one realises that one had actually meant to convey so many other good things about the person. But '*is*' is final. So one says, 'she is also...'. And so on, endlessly adding but at each addition one is admitting that what was said before was not as final as was indicated. So, one is also amending.

5

Rent Appropriation and Capitalist Occupation

A Lot of Theory

Apparently the objectives of the World Bank are quite different from those of the IMF and WTO. It often appears that the principal desire of the Bank is to help the poor, even by establishing productive enterprises outside the organisational rules of capital. So, in order to understand the place of the Bank within the overall framework of global capital, we will extend the frontiers of the theoretical space, which we have already fenced off. We had seen that the process of primitive capital accumulation is not primitive in any chronological sense. Capital earns profits on the basis of market transactions based on capitalist property and contract laws. At the same time, capital also enjoys rent disguised as profit. This it can extract because it possesses productive resources, control over markets, knowledge[1] and science. In the era of globalisation, the principal arms of big capital in its campaign for occupation of these territories are the IMF and WTO. But the dependence of global capital on the World Bank is by no means less than its reliance on IMF and WTO. Only, it is of a different order.

In our view, the determining character of capitalism in the age of globalisation is the curtailment of economic sovereignty of nation states, particularly of the poor nations. (The specific ways in which the real discrimination between poor and rich nation states is effected will be elaborated upon later.) The denial of sovereignty involves the abrogation of the right of the national government to decide domestic economic policies and policies relating to international transactions. It also involves the abolition or modification of certain laws and regulations. Such laws and regulations include laws relating to the economy (property, contract, right to trade, right to adjudicate in case of economic offences) and rules relating to economic relations. Of course, those who have given currency to the term in the current context attribute a benevolent connotation to it. They are totally silent about its aggressive designs. The meaning that they tout is 'unrestricted flow of capital and commodities'. Ensuring such free flow itself entails a thorough change of laws, regulations and an administrative set-up. But this freedom itself is a discriminatory freedom. There are various kinds of exemptions, depending on what is advantageous to the rich countries. Even those in governmental authority often resent such changes. So, in order to compel poor countries to accept these changes, regular economic warfare and, if necessary, military campaigns have to be launched. Understandably, those who tout globalisation today are totally silent about these aspects.

Through sustained pressure, global capital (i.e. large MNCs) takes possession of the sites of knowledge, culture, nature, markets, and even the games that people think they play, the world over. Capital uses its occupancy to extract rent disguised as profit. That is, capital earns both profit and rent disguised as profit.

This commonplace observation has immense theoretical connotations. Traditional Marxists believe in a certain kind of historical evolution. They think that capitalism was established by negating (the negation of) feudalism. In plain words, feudalism collapsed under the upsurge of hope for a better society; and out of the synthesis of this hope and the constraints of reality was born capitalism. In countries like ours, the transition was not completed because of the colonial past, so the story goes. Searching for the reasons for this difference constitutes a large area of research. But if, in reality, capital extracts rent on the basis of occupancy rights, just like feudal rights were used in the past, the so-called difference ceases to be as important as one believed.

Let us examine the significance of monopoly control over markets. On the basis of this control, capital can manipulate prices. As a result, the prices of commodities purchased by capitalist enterprises from non-capitalist enterprises are fixed at levels such that almost the entire surplus produced outside the capitalist sector (for example, within the cottage industry sector) is appropriated by the capitalist sector as rent. The relation between rent, product price and who will appropriate the surplus needs some elaboration.

One can imagine competitive capitalism as a system within which labourers get wages sufficient to meet their basic needs, and the surplus is so distributed that capital earns the same rate of profit in all sectors. These two rules determine the rate of profit and the relative prices. But this depiction is silent about rent. By establishing one's claims over the right to produce and trade, surplus is appropriated as rent. Suppose the price of cloth is fixed at Rs.150 per metre on the basis of minimum wages and average rate of profit. Now let us think of an alternative system in which cloth is manufactured in only one enterprise. This monopoly enterprise increases the pricc of cloth to Rs.200 per metre. Since there are no alternative sources, buyers are forced to buy at the enhanced price. Monopoly capital extracts Rs.50 worth of rent per metre. This process also changes the relative prices of commodities. One could put it thus: the level of colonisation, or extent of control over market, becomes one of the determinants of price.

Let us try to understand, with the aid of an example, how surplus generated by production outside capitalist organisations can also be appropriated as rent by capital. Composite mills once dominated the Indian textile industry. Weaving, dyeing, polishing, etc. were all done within the same mill. Now such mills have almost disappeared. There are many instances where the power looms are hired out to those who previously worked on them as labourers. Now these labourers-turned-owners produce mostly with their own and their family labour. Such units supply cloth on orders from large mills against advances of costs. The mills only dye and polish the cloth thus acquired. The amount earned by these 'independent, self-employed, producers' is certainly less than what they used to earn as permanent labourers in the mills, hour for hour, taking into consideration all the statutory benefits that they enjoyed as permanent employees in the organised sector. When they have orders on hand, their monthly family earnings may be more than that of a mill worker. This is because the earnings are no longer just the payments for the individual labour of the mill worker; other family members also work in the unit now. Besides, there is no limit on the hours worked. No question of respecting factory laws. The large mills have monopoly control over the cloth market. In many cases, the cloth-making unit is tied to the mills through a system of debts and advances – a sort of hypothecation. This debt-advance chain further reduces competition in the market in which the weaving unit sells its cloth. By paying low price to these weaving units, the large mills manage to appropriate almost the entire surplus produced in this cottage production sector, in the form of rent.

It is not as if big capital sucks rent only out of concerns to which it puts out work. It even extracts rent from such enterprises with which it does not, apparently, have any connection. Capital appropriates surplus as rent even from those who inhabit the margins, the interstices of capitalist production like the itinerant carpenter-bagman, the small electrical mechanic, the menial working in the homes of those who can 'afford' to employ them, and even the house spouse – those who inhabit the extensive network of gaps and fissures that make up the subcity[2] of capitalism that goes on serving the city of gentleman's capitalism, silently and secretly. Often, those who employ them or otherwise enjoy the benefit of their services do not have the ability to pay for the full value of these services. One can put it thus: the surplus produced by these marginalised producers is appropriated by the capitalist enterprise, which pays low wages to the buyers of these services. That is, the capitalist enterprise pays wages lower than that necessary to buy what are considered to be basic requirements at prices determined by competitive capitalism. The enterprise can do this because a part of the basic requirements of the worker is purchased from the marginalised sector at prices, which are lower than competitive market prices.[3] The surplus produced in the agricultural sector is also appropriated by big capital by using its control over both the market for inputs of the agricultural sector made by the industrial sector and the market for the inputs supplied by the agricultural sector to the industrial sector. It uses this control to set prices in such a way that a large part of agricultural sector's surplus is siphoned off by the industrial sector.

Big capital does not extract rent only through its control over markets. By suspending common rights over land, forest and water, and by establishing private property rights over such non-produced inputs also, it can extract rent. Rent is also extracted by exercising private property rights over knowledge, science, technology, seeds, etc. after these have been transformed into marketable commodities. The process of transforming these into marketable commodities is also primitive capital accumulation.[4] And, for extracting rent using the ownership of these resources it does not matter whether these inputs are employed in capitalist enterprises or cooperative enterprises or peasant agriculture.

The point to be underlined is that there is no reason why global capital should invest in the project of expanding the borders of capitalist production to include all productive activity, when it can well appropriate surplus from other forms of production organisation. In fact, it is desirable to exclude many sectors from capitalist production. It is then easier to force the workforce to labour under inhuman conditions. That is, they can be made to labour under conditions, which the ethics, norms and laws of capitalist enterprise recognise to be 'inhuman'. Which kind of productive activities will be brought directly under capital's organisational control, and which will be left outside for extraction of surplus in the form of rent depends on economic, political, and technological factors. One of the economic conditions is productivity. To extract surplus at an average rate from sectors where productivity is low, workers in this sector have to be compelled to work for longer hours, than is the rule, at average wages. This is difficult within organised capitalist enterprise. It is therefore desirable to exclude such sectors from the ambit of an organised factory system. The size of the market and the local concentration of buyers for a particular product or service may also be important.[5] Consider the great rush of globalised capital to capture the retail sector. The business of the neighbourhood shopkeeper was quite secure from aggressive encroachment by supermarket chains as long as the turnover did not promise to justify the large investment of supermarket business.

There may be political reasons too for excluding some sector from the productive segment directly organised by capitalist principles. One of the principal political reasons is the organisational strength of the workers. Capital does not have to confront the strength of the workers if a particular productive sector can be excluded from the factory system. Whether such exclusion is feasible depends to a large extent on the prevailing technological conditions.

In the current age of information technology, it is possible to instantly transmit information relating to demand or orders, and instructions relating to production, from one corner of the globe to another. This is one of the factors which helps explain the fact that while centralisation of production was the major tendency of capital up to the 1980s, the current trend is towards fragmentation of the production process and parcelling out parts of the process for production outside the central organisation on a putting out basis. Works like collating information, accounting, advertising, marketing, editing, etc. are being increasingly put out by the central capitalist organisation.

In this inordinately long section we have, *so far, reached three conclusions* that are important from our perspective. *First,* within an economy controlled by capital, capital cannot only tolerate production outside capitalist enterprise, but may even make space for such production in capital's very own interest. *Second,* capital dominates non-capitalist enterprise and uses such dominance to extract part or whole of the surplus produced by them as rent. Of course, such rent is not visible in the accounts. It is disguised as profit or rental (i.e. charges for hiring out property), or some such specie of payment. *Third*, the presence of rent makes prices indeterminate. This third conclusion may appear to be strange to those with even an elementary knowledge of bourgeois economics. So let us elaborate.

Bourgeois economics says that rent is not price determining but price determined. That is it is not rent that determines price, but price that determines rent. There is some logic in this. Rent is not an element of cost in the same sense as raw material cost; wage payments and profit are constitutive of costs. The latter are essential elements of capitalist cost calculation, while rent is not. So rent does not determine price in the same way as these other payments do. The normal price per unit of production is determined by the cost of wages, fuel, raw material, etc. per unit of output, together with the profit at normal (or average) rate on these costs. The additional price that can be obtained is rent. We would look at it in a different way: it is because rent is extracted on the basis of various kinds of monopoly that commodities have to be sold at prices above the necessary cost of capitalist production. If price is somewhere more than the normal capitalist cost of production, somewhere else it is bound to be lower. In a sense, this is simply a definitional statement, or a statement that must always hold. The sum of the normal capitalist cost of production in all lines of production taken together is the total value of output produced in that economy. This is what must be distributed as various elements of cost, including rent. So, if in some line of production more is claimed on the basis of the rent extracted in that line of production, somewhere else less will be available for distribution as cost. For example, the low-wage employee is buying the service of the house-worker at less than the normal price. To elaborate: the employee is receiving less than the competitive market determined cost of reproduction of the hours worked by that employee. And the employee is paying less than the normal capitalist cost of production of the housework that he or she is purchasing. This lower price is the source of rent in the enterprise where the employee works. The employee is paid less than normal wage so the cost of production of that capitalist enterprise is lower than normal, but the commodity is selling at normal price (i.e. at a price sufficient to pay the normal cost of production). The excess of the normal price (which is also the price at which the product sells in the market) over its actual cost of production is rent. The distribution of rent and the values of relative prices depend on the relative intensities of monopoly control over markets exercised by different fractions of capital, and the distribution of monopoly rights over resources among these fractions. In this sense, the continued existence of rent within the capitalist system makes the system indeterminate. The example of the monopoly producer of cloth showed that rent leads to indeterminate relative prices of commodities. Or perhaps one may put it thus: even from a superficial angle (i.e. without considering the in depth what constitutes prices) one can see that relative prices are not determined by the so-called scientific laws of demand and supply; they are determined by the distribution of economic control or power.

At the margins of the capitalist system, the outcasts of development appear to be accommodated as self-employed. Like the fisherman, the carpenter-bagman, the odd-job man who also specialises in repairing huts, the house-worker, etc. This list could also include the marginal farmer. It is also possible to accommodate them in non-capitalist productive organisations like cooperatives where production is socialised (as distinct from individual productive organisations like those run by the self employed) keeping capital's surplus extraction unabated. Such peaceful coexistence is even possible with feudal production organisations.

If one looks at the significance of rent within the capitalist system from a slightly different angle, one can see that it imparts flexibility to the system. If you take a superficial view, you will imagine that capital is leaving certain areas of the economy to non-capital out of magnanimity or under duress. It is as if this is not pure capital but a distortion, which fits into the structure of the third world or the one-time colonies. But from the analysis of capitalist rent, it can be understood that there is no purity of capital. Impure rent hides itself in pure profit. So the difference is one of degree, not of the basic structure. How much space will be allowed to noncapital depends on the concrete conditions. We have seen how economic, political, and technological conditions influence this decision. (At the level of the broader perspective of philosophy, of course, the absence of purity, of self-sufficiency, of being self-evident of any system is a commonplace since post-modernism[6] gained currency).

The significance of the so-called informal sector can perhaps best be explored in this light. Marx discussed PCA principally in the context of dispossession of peasant rights.[7] A similar phenomenon is today generating a lot of deserved public condemnation – the seizure of peasants' rights by state governments to acquire land for industrialisation. This has become a major focus of anti-government agitation in the 'Left Front' ruled state of West Bengal. Farmers – comprising medium and small landowners, sharecroppers, and agricultural labourers – have been forcibly evicted from their hearth and fields with such brutality that even the coalition partners of the largest left party, the CPI(M), have been forced to cry foul. To many, this appears to be the result of just the caprice of the Chief Minister who had committed the state to providing prime agricultural land to the Tatas at a place called Singur for construction of an automobile company. The fact is more sinister.

The process of acquisition of agricultural land is simultaneously the process of converting the peasants into refugees of development. From independent peasants they are transformed into the marginalised immigrants to the urban centres who may get some jobs in the 'informal sector' if they are lucky. This sector supplies services for the privileged segments working in the organised sector, like menial service in the houses, odd support services like electrical wiring, ironing, taking the mobile- (and sometimes gun) toting kids to school, etc. Acquisition of prime agricultural land for industrial ventures serves a dual purpose. On the one hand, the cost of development of infrastructure is minimised, because the crops produced on such lands must have had access to roads. Water, which is required in substantial amounts in many industrial ventures, must also have been easily available. On the other hand, the displaced will flock to the estates built on their lands to crowd the informal sector there. Their surplus will be readily extracted as rent by the MNC to which the land is handed over. These refugees of development will provide cheap support services to the employees in the organised sector, which is built on land from which the peasants have been displaced. The organised sector can, therefore, pay lower wages than if these services had to be purchased from the organised sector. Thus this sector can appropriate the surplus originating in the informal sector, this appropriation is in the form of rent.

The World Bank often appears to be opposed to globalised capital because it works in the space of negotiation between capital and non-capital. In reality, taking advantage of the flexibility of capital, the World Bank tries to mediate between capital and non-capital so as to maintain the stability of the existing order keeping the dominance of global capital intact. It is not even as if this mediation by the Bank buys stability at the cost of profit of global capital. As we have seen in the context of land acquisition by the government, non-capital's surplus (i.e. the surplus produced by the marginalised, self-employed service provider or the menial) actually bloats the 'profits' of the formal capitalist sector.

The idea of contradiction or compromise appears to be out of place in the popular perception of capitalism. The idea that capital has to compromise with non-capitalist producers or with the outcastes of capitalist growth, so that a sufficient dominance can be maintained for rent appropriation, does not gel with the notion of purity of capital. At a particular juncture of the history of the West, the lore of logical self-sufficiency of capitalism and modernism crystallised. And the characters of this myth strut about in the media, in the writings of hired or infantile politicians and economists, and in popular art and literature. This makes it difficult to accept that at the base of the capitalist system there is illogic, absence of reason and instability, just as in any exploitative order. This also reduces the visibility of coercion, which is as much necessary for maintaining the stability of this order, as it is for maintaining the stability any order.

A Piece of History

Historians claim that a blend of the pronounced discrimination of slave society and the principles of equality of an older tribal order formed the basis of Western feudal society. Though hereditary, family-based social and economic discrimination formed the core of the relation between the aristocrats and the exploited people, the principles of kingship were circumscribed and monitored by the expectations of the community. The stability of the feudal system would be in jeopardy if feudal exploitation crossed these limits.

This description is generally accepted, so it is recognised that in the period just preceding capitalism in the West, in spite of the dominance of the aristocrats, the expectation of the subjects influenced the principles of kingship. But capitalist culture breeds the illusion that there is no space for uncertainty and compromise within the system. Logic is the sole basis of this order. Everything is certain, determined by the logic of the marketplace. Since there is no indeterminacy, the question of compromise does not arise within this order. If, within the state structure of this system there are pulls and pressures, this indicates that there are residuals of older orders or displacements of such orders into baseless dreams of future orders. Such are likely to occur in the third world countries. But in the West, where capitalism has flowered in all its glory, in its purest incarnation, the economy is controlled by the inviolable logic of private ownership and market. Our position is that this geo-political difference is a lie born of the imperialist culture of Western capitalism.

Revolt against exploitation based on hereditary status was at the core of the uprising against Western feudalism. Just as the rising bourgeois, lacking social status, joined the movement; so also did the lowest of the low – the bondsmen, those who were tied down to definite plots, with no right to move out. All were opposed to inequality based on principles of hereditary social status. But the equality desired by the serf differed radically from the equality for which the bourgeois fought. The discipline of the community and the social stratification of the feudal system were intimately connected, so a revolt against hierarchical rights was also, by implication, a revolt against the traditional community. Consequently, a certain image of individualism and an attraction towards it emerged in the course of the revolt.

When the battle was over, a new order was established under the rule of capital. In time, a specific notion of individual liberties and equality was internalised by its culture. It was the notion which was consistent with the rule of capital. New mythologies supportive of the new rule and exploitation emerged. The paeans in praise of free market are but an expression of the modernised, fashionable versions of these myths. The notion of individual freedom, of course, played a progressive role in opposition to the discipline of the community in the anti-feudal struggle. Through many battles, independence-loving people had won the right to logically argue against the illogic of feudal discipline, against feudal opposition to science. But when stability returned under a new order of authority and exploitation, the notion of individualism worked in the service of the new exploitative class.

Capitalist lore surrounding the new independent individual, taking great pride in the newfound equality, mushroomed everywhere. With the birth of the print press, this became a veritable explosion. Assortment of folktales about the independent, self-respecting individual who could achieve anything (with no inheritance!) began to be imagined. Rich man's daughter weds honest son of poor parents, or the other way round. Justice is done to the poorest of the poor. And so much else. Derivatives of the principal themes of independence and equality were expressed in different forms at the various sites of social interaction.

At the site of the discourse about the economy, the principal characters in the myth are the buyer and seller. Qualitatively they are all equal. Everyone can acquire property by purchasing in the market. All can enter into contracts for exchanging property. In contrast, in feudal society specific individuals have specific rights. In the mythical capitalist economy, the scientific laws of demand and supply working through sale and purchase of commodities decide production, distribution and employment. There is no direct relation between person and person. In this myth, such relations are mediated by commodity exchange in the market. As God was once the origin of all activity, today Markets determine all economic action. There is no place for community or classes. Those who talk of classes, or some such, want to dupe the people in order to fulfill some hidden agenda.

As a matter of fact, community or class conflict is not so visible in everyday life as it is in societies based clearly on classes with differentiated rights. But our analysis of the apparently self-sufficient, determinate market system has revealed that for capitalist markets to work, specific rights over inputs (natural resources, stock of knowledge, etc.) and right to trade have to be ordained. Such rights are not determined through any market process and thus not through any 'logical' process. Specific individuals or organisations seize such rights with brute force, state power, and such other. The horizons of knowledge are broadened in the course of capitalist growth. New fields of science, technology and natural resources are discovered. Again there is a struggle to redefine the legal system to establish ownership over these. It is in this sense that we have said that the process of primitive capital accumulation is incomplete, never to be completed.

The existence of capitalist rent proves the incompleteness of capital's logic, the uncertainty of outcome of the capitalist system. The quantum and distribution of capitalist rent is not dependent on the logic of the market. It depends purely on coercion. The distribution of rent again determines relative prices. Rather, one should say that the same distribution of coercive strength, which determines rent allocation, also determines relative prices. Hence, we would underscore in spite of repetition: the capitalist system like (just like the pre-capitalist systems), cannot be bound and sealed by impersonal laws alone.

Rent is extracted on the basis of rights over what is not produced by human labour (e.g. water, forests, land) or what is produced by undefined community labour (e.g. the stock of knowledge of a society). Such rights are not established through the so-called logical rules of the market (though once established such rights are tradable in the market). Hence, such rights can be used to extract the surplus from non-capitalist societies also. Whether this possibility will be realised depends on a number of conditions, some of which we have discussed.

New contradictions are generated if non-capitalist enterprise is accommodated within the economy. Self-employed destitutes of development have expectations and demands, which differ from those of both workers and owners of capital. Again, those who work under putting out arrangements have different demands. They all evolve different cultures and aspirations. So, to maintain stability of the system, keeping its dominance intact, capital mutates in different ways.

We do not mean to imply that capital is the thinking subject that decides the course of events. We have purposely chosen the imagery of mutation. It is an articulated process comprising the environment and elemental aspects of the organic entity. It is not as if capitalists conspire as a body and act according to a plan. If the concrete is such that it warrants expansion of the field of capital, then suitable cultural justifications are generated for such aggrandising growth. If, on the other hand, the prevailing socio-economic conditions are such that it is more acceptable or more profitable to accommodate non-capitalist enterprise, the prevailing culture will find justifications for this. For example, one may talk of reforms with a human face. Or, under different circumstances, one may talk of the need to 'cut out the flab' by 'rationalising' workforce (which is a euphemism which has lost its impact because everyone recognises what this call signifies – the beginning of a new phase of reduction of workforce).

One face of capitalism is a severe, ruthless individualistic culture, which germinated in the course of the conflict between community and capital. This culture is embedded in Western religious values. Today it finds an equally forceful expression in its hysteric obsession with forcing its individualistic values on alien cultures. The Western nation states can, therefore, adopt a righteous attitude even when invading other nations under pretexts that are known to be false. And a large segment of the population buys it! At the same time, apparently a more humane culture springs from the ground of conflict-compromise and dominance through compromise and persuasion. In fact, the two sets of cultural values complement/supplement each other to weave a web of illusion-seduction in the aid of maintaining capital's dominance in the age of globalisation. Those engaged in dissimulating global capital's domination are themselves caught up in this web: the economist extolling the virtues of liberalisaton, the 'popular' litterateurs, film makers, and so on. This is not to deny entirely the persuasive power of recognition and material gains that are on offer to the economist or the culture specialist who accepts the ideological premise of self-sufficiency of individualism!

This myth is a way of perceiving reality, which works in the service of status quo. It presents the system sans conflict, working in a way that is inevitable and efficient, determined by scientific laws. Myth making is a means of internalising coercion in every society, of obliterating the element of coercion from conscious perception. Our understanding of capitalism, built up through an analysis of capitalist rent, is that it is based on unending expansionism. This insatiable urge makes it necessary that, at this juncture of the history of capital, the entire world should be brought under a uniform legal and administrative system, a standardised method for establishing proprietary control over resources, together with a homogeneous set of economic policies. This is the stuff of imperialism in the age of globalisation. Strong-arm tactics, like applying persistent economic pressure and launching military campaigns, like the Iraq war under any old pretext are the order of the day, rather than debates and discussions.

It is quite unlikely that a vast segment of the American population will suddenly be caught up in a frenzy of nationalist fervour, supporting a war-mongering Bush and flooding the nation with national flags because it serves the structural requirements of capitalism. This structural necessity is articulated by a harsh value system and the accompanying ethics. In summary fashion, it can be labelled as a White, Male, Christian value system. It is this morality that motivates the crusades of globalisation, whether it takes the form of military campaigns against dissenters or the form of incessant economic pressure for reforming the legal system or changing economic policies. This ethics and morality is by no means less harsh than feudal discipline. This value system preaches that subsidies, relief, and unemployment dole cultivate lethargy and reduce the motivation to work. In the absence of international aid, for example, the poor of the underdeveloped nations would be forced into adopting the 'efficient', individualistic value system of the Christian world.[8] Common rights (e.g. over land, water, forests, knowledge) make people unenterprising. Without private ownership, proper allocation of resources cannot be ensured. Minimum wage legislation and trade union rights, which violate the principles of individual freedom, are the result of trade union pressures and should abrogated. The ancient right holders, like the *adivasis*, who are being displaced by modern projects like the erection of large dams, are facing this predicament because of their inability to properly utilise nature according to the demands of the markets. It is therefore unethical to undertake any special project for their relief. It is unfair to give any special privilege to any backward segment of the population, as individual intellectual brilliance is then not appropriately rewarded. With the growth of capitalism, this unyielding form of individualism began to crystallise. This rigid individualism was internalised by the strand of Christian religious consciousness, which had already identified itself with the struggle for individual liberties against the feudal discipline of the community. In time, this became the ruling, White orthodoxy. This was the bourgeois value system which William Simon, the US Treasury Secretary, had evoked while arguing in favour of imposing stringent economic discipline on the British government in 1976. He had clearly stated that bourgeois ethics and morality were the stakes in the debate surrounding the imposition of these conditions on Britain. This aggressive, almost religious ideology gives birth to an equally violent nationalism: My values are the best. My country is the bearer of these values. Thus begin the crusades of the age of globalisation.

The specific situation determines the form of warfare. Just

as military campaigns are a form of warfare, so also the use of international economic pressure to bring a country to its knees, is a form of warfare in this new age of global capital. Generally, the patrons of globalisation, like the IMF and WTO untiringly carry on the second form of imperialist aggression. If, in spite of so much economic pressure, a country continues to be recalcitrant, the US Marines are forced to launch mortal crusades to punish the infidels, by time-honoured principles of warfare.

An uncompromising, rigid, individualistic value system is one expression of bourgeois ethics. But the capitalist system cannot be sustained solely on the basis of a specific form of individualism bred on the bourgeois notion of equality. Pre-existing rights are abrogated and a particular kind of private rights established through the process of primitive capital accumulation. Capital extracts rent on the basis of such occupancy. Capital can countenance non-capital within the system as it can extract surplus from this sector in the form of rent. Not only that, capital stands to gain by leaving certain productive activities, or parts of it, to non-capitalist enterprise. Since there is space for non-capitalist enterprise, classes other than capitalist and working class co-exist with these two classes. To pre-existing classes are added the refugees of capitalist development. They have their specific desires, and demands from the state. Through a process of accommodation and symbiosis, keeping intact the dominance of the ethics of capital and individualism, a different kind of bourgeois ethics emerges – one, which is essential for sustaining capital's hegemony within this conjuncture. This mutated bourgeois ethics again influences the ethics of the exploited and oppressed through a process of accommodation.

Economic theory, like all social 'science' theories, is a component of culture. Dominant or orthodox theories are part of the 'ideological state apparatus'. The unyielding individualistic bourgeois ethics that we have mentioned, has its correlate at the site of economic theory in the shape of the theories whose elementary agency is the own utility maximising individual. As the hegemonic culture mutates, so does economic theory, as an aspect of culture. The mutated economic theory, which helps sustain the dominance of capital in the changed context, develops along apparently different trajectories. In the course of our discussion of primitive capital accumulation, in Chapter 2, we had schematically discussed the process of transformation of community consciousness. Through primitive capital accumulation communities lose their ancient rights. The structure of community is changed radically. The displaced individuals lose their traditional community identity. Individuals who previously had separate community identities converge to urban settlements to eke out an existence on the margins of the development process. In the changed context, new communities are born. New collectives have different kinds of demands. They demand increased government expenditure on healthcare, education, and social security, for instance. In the neoclassical theory, born of pure bourgeois individualism, such expenditure is unjustified. Such expenditure by government leads to a production pattern that violates the dictates of market demand generated by individual preferences and an income distribution decided by the wisdom of the market. However, as we have seen in Chapters 2 and 3, by introducing the concept of 'social benefit', a concept derived eclectically from the inchoate conceptual/perceptual field referred to as common sense, arguments in favour of social welfare expenditure can be accommodated within the structure of standard neoclassical theory. The logic of social benefits finds expression in newer forms in the writings of the liberal economists. Scientific or unquestionable criteria of evaluation of social benefits based on the logic of the market are impossible. Using this recognised gap in market logic, liberal economists like Amartya Sen import some attractive criteria of social desirability based on their personal preferences. Such supplements to orthodox theory win accolades at the international level. Statistics based on such criteria are used by the UNO to rank nations according to level of development. Thus we have criteria like the Human Development Index, the Quality of Life Index, and so on.

Establishment economics finds an escape hatch to modify itself, to maintain its ideological hegemony now standing on the high moral ground of concern for development of humanity. Its categories and structure of argument remain unchanged, only at the margin a specific distribution of government expenditure is accommodated. The responsibility of applying these so-called path-breaking theoretical insights to the real world rests with the World Bank. So the World Bank is reborn as the benevolent incarnation of global capital.

Development economics has played a significant role in inducing some rethinking on economic policy through the World Bank. There is no discursive space for poverty, famines and such, within the rigorous field of the neoclassical theory. Reality of a market economy is logical, according to uncompromising individualist culture. So, there is no reason to be perturbed by any event. That thousands of cotton farmers in Vidarbha have committed suicide, unable to cope with poverty and indebtedness, is of no concern to theorists in this rigid mould. After all, they were speculating like good market operators. That their speculations did not work out warrants no special consideration. In contrast, economists like Sen are specifically concerned with such issues. A point that warrants reiteration: neither the mutation of the economy under the dominance of global capital, nor the mutation of the culture of capital is the result of some huge conspiracy. There is no meta-subject. In small ways we all contribute to the ideology of status quo. You 'belong' to a poor country. You have grown up in a culture where a sense of community was pervasive. As a global economist you practise the mystical 'science' of individual choice (and thence, social choice). And you believe in market price as the great homogeniser. But as you commute between the geographical spaces of the rich and the poor countries, your mind too flits uncomfortably between different cognitive fields. You see the poverty, squalor and the ignorance in which the majority in the country of your birth live. Some simply forget. They numb their cognitive faculties by assuming some evolutionary perspective. But the more acute can avoid schizophrenia only by assuming a position of benevolence. Individual freedom to choose in markets, uninhibited by any bigbrotherly interference by the state is all right, but you also have to think of the individual not just as an actor in the market, but as a living human. Questions of life, and so of death, are unthinkable within the space of neoclassical economics, because the one who chooses lacks any other attribute than the ability to independently choose. Consideration of life cannot be accommodated within the discursive space of neoclassical economics. Actually, the individual as an entity is absent in neoclassical economics other than as *The Great Optimising Chooser*. But your catholic mind sees fragmentary images of the poverty of the half that dies every day, from its other cognitive field. So, to basic needs and questions of access, of empowerment.[9] You cannot but be hopeful that the state or some benevolent *avatar* of global capital will do this tinkering. You assume the mantle of conscience keeper. You preach, you begin to believe in the possibility of the system to reform itself. But when you are confronted with the choice between the great homogenising march of global capital and the demand of life and livelihood of the local who is a potential refugee of development, you have no doubt about the efficacy of globalisation.[10]

The benevolence of the neighbourhood shopkeeper towards beggars varies directly with the intensity of the shopkeeper's demands from his God. Development economics was most acclaimed in the 1950s and 1960s when the Cold War between the socialist world and the 'free world' was at its peak. Socialist ideas were gradually penetrating the poor countries. The capitalist world was forced to think of measures that would reduce poverty while keeping capital's dominance intact so that people's anger could be tempered.

In today's world, capitalism has no such fear. But the rate at which poverty, unemployment, death from hunger and malnutrition are growing, there is the ever-increasing threat of chaos and terrorism, to counter the terror unleashed by capitalism, spreading to all corners of the globe. So capital is again actively trying to apply the balm of development economics through the World Bank. The Bank talks of conferring legal proprietary rights on the forest dwellers and marginal farmers. It insists on the need for decentralising of planning and for people's participation at village-level planning. It urges the end of social and state discrimination against the poor. It tells the governments to include the marginalised and the outcasts within the administrative structure of the government.

Some of the palliatives are just eyewash, with no possibility of implementation. Take, for instance, the advice to end discriminatory behaviour. There is no recognition of social discrimination. So its decrease cannot also be officially seen. Temporarily, there may be some spread of community-based or cooperative-based production as a result of conferring legal proprietorship to forest dwellers and marginal farmers. In most cases this is likely to be a passing phenomenon, as has been seen in the case of most land reform measures adopted even in states that are ruled by those who profess leftism. Conferring legal rights on forests to the dwellers may even be a step towards concentration of ownership by capital.[11] To the extent that these forms of production persist, capital will have to extract surplus from such enterprise as rent through its control over the markets. In neither case does capital cease to hold sway.

But some of the reforms promoted by the World Bank have more significant effects. This is possible because there is no purity in capital's policy or in its culture. Capital mutates in response to the expectations of the dominated. The hopes and aspirations of such groups also undergo transformation. When the Sardar Sarovar Project was launched, the first demand of the forest dwellers, facing eviction, was that the plan to construct a dam must be scrapped as the forests would be submerged and they would lose their lives and livelihood. The Narmada Bachao Andolan had threatened that the villagers would court *jal samadhi.*[12] They would wait in their village, at the temple of Sulpaneshwari Devi, to be submerged by the advancing waters of the river Narmada, as the height of the dam was gradually raised beyond that of their villages. The dam was constructed and the temple of Sulpaneshwari Devi was submerged. No one courted *jal samadhi*. The forest dwellers were displaced and became the refugees of development – the outcasts of capitalism. The very identity of the community changed. This was reflected in the change in the demand of the Narmada Baachao Andolan

– from no dam to rehabilitation and compensation for the ousted. The World Bank invests in large dams (and also disassociates itself from such projects in the face of public pressure!). It is also active in rehabilitation projects. The relatively autonomous forest dwellers lose their identity and are transformed into homeless marginalised under the complete sway of capital. Globalised capital materialises in its benevolent form to organise and finance their rehabilitation.

In this way, through a process of evolution, global capital responds to changes by adapting its tactics, strategy and even its culture. But the dominance of capital is not curbed. If one takes a superficial view, without understanding capital's project and the manner of appropriating surplus, some of the policies of the Bank may appear to violate the basic character of capital. This is the greatest achievement of the Bank. Now the left in power also says there is no harm in taking World Bank loan if it is for some project that they have 'independently' chosen. They become quite maudlin if the Bank showers praise on the performance of the government run by them.

NOTES

1. This is not a familiar way of looking at the problem of intellectual properties, but I do not think this way of treating the problem violates the basic idea of primitive capital accumulation. Primitive capital accumulation abolishes common rights and establishes bourgeois property rights. Knowledge is a resource that was typically considered as belonging to the community. After all, no intellectual product can be born either out of nothing, or out of resources for which payment has been made. To take a facile example, the inventor or 'creator' always works through a given language (verbal, mathematical, whatever). And language is always part of the common cultural tool bag of a society. We will discuss these issues in somewhat greater detail in the next chapter.
2. ....'cause no one would like to admit
   that there is a city underground
   where people live every day
   off the waste and decay
   off the discards of their fellowman
   here in subcity life is hard

we can't receive any government relief
Tracy Chapman, *Subcity,* album: Crossroads; 1989.

3. This may be one way of looking at the phenomenon of the so-called informal sector and its utility to global capital.
4. Conventionally, one does not include the process of establishing private property rights over these resources within what is called primitive capital accumulation. But to my mind, any extension of private property rights which furthers future (capitalist rent extraction disguised as) profit accumulation through the working of the market, warrants being treated as primitive capital accumulation
5. A student-friend, Soumendra Chattopadhyay, pointed this out to me.
6. Post-modernism is a way of thinking which, as the name suggests, succeeded the modern way of thinking. Modernity, as opposed to the previous modes of thought, was immensely confident about the potential of logical thought. It believed that all necessary and meaningful knowledge could be derived strictly by applying logical principles. Post-modernism argues that this is a hollow claim. It comes to this conclusion chiefly because, as they show through the examination of modern pieces that claim to be rigorously based on logical premises and arguments, logic itself is complemented by rhetorical or metaphysical arguments or assumptions. The post-modernists claim that every logical system is inevitably rooted in articles of faith. The most celebrated example of this critique is post-modernism's criticism of structural linguistics. Structural linguistics had claimed to have put linguistics on a thoroughly logical footing, through its twin propositions that words are arbitrary and that words mean only in difference. That we call this table a 'table' is purely arbitrary. There is no organic link between the image of the table and the linguistic sign 'table'. In this sense, words are arbitrary. Further, this linguistic sign, or word, conjures up an image that is comprehensible only because it is different from other images – say, the image of the chair. The linguistic-phonetic sign 'chair' is, similarly, recognisable only in its difference from other such signs. These two propositions together, however have the unsolicited effect of establishing that all meaning is conventional: the categories of thought and communication together with the visual and/or phonetic signifiers of these categories are all part of the cultural conventions of a given society. So what is conveyed is hardly what the sender of the message wants to convey. And,

even more frightening, one cannot even think articulately what one wants to covey. So the figure of the author is just a rhetorical device, a faith, or an instrument of cultural control: some use the figure of the author to establish their authority to divine what the author actually said. The structural linguists, most prominently Saussure, used another rhetorical device to get out of this uncomfortable realisation. They put speech before writing, implying that somehow the intention of the author was directly or transparently present in the spoken word, that it is self-evident, which was not so in the case of the written word. This opened up structural linguistics to another criticism: if speech were purely subjective – conveying the intention of the speaker - then it would not make sense to the listener. It makes sense only because it is a string of conventional audible signs. Which makes it just a species of writing. So we have writing before speech: a reversal of hierarchy, which goes by the quaint name of deconstruction. See Sturrock, J., 2002.

7. Marx, K., 1959: 673, 676, etc.
8. This attitude is reflected in so many tracts and in so diverse areas of economic theory and policy that it makes annotation impossible. One fertile territory that the interested reader may search for suitable quotes is 'foreign aid'. One of the most consistent promoters of the White, Male, Christian ideology, particularly in the area of economic aid, was Milton Friedman. Way back in1958, when the perceived threat of the spread of communist ideology was inclining opinion in the West towards the need for using foreign aid as a means of retaining the loyalty of the erstwhile colonies, Friedman was consistently opposing any 'charitable' transfer of resources. His opposition was based on his reading that aid would promote greater governmental activity replacing individual risk taking. This would further reduce growth potential in these countries, as the greatest impediment to growth was the absence of the Western individualistic value system. To establish his position, Friedman refuted various arguments that were being advanced in favour of foreign aid, with scant respect to history. One of these was the argument that

   'the underdeveloped countries are too poor to save and provide capital for themselves. Here too the alleged fact is most dubious. Currently developed countries were once underdeveloped. Whence came their capital? (Friedman, Milton, 1958, p. 69)... What is required in the underdeveloped countries is the release of the energies of millions of able, active, and vigorous people *who have been chained by ignorance, custom and tradition.'* (ibid, p.71, italics added.)

The forgetfulness of Friedman erases the history of plunder of the colonies that provided capital for the development of the 'currently developed countries'. But leave that aside. The issue that we wish to highlight is that there has always been a substantial body of 'respectable' public opinion that has argued that it is the presence/absence of the individualistic value system that can explain differences in the rates of growth between nations.

9. The reference is to Sen of HDI. The Capabilities Approach is less operational and more responsive to heterogeneity that the market cannot capture, based as it is on the principle of homogenisation through prices.
10. After a lot of tantalising prevarication, Amartya Sen came out forcefully in support of the West Bengal state government in the still ongoing debate between the supporters of the government, bent on acquiring land from the peasants for setting up industry, and those fighting for the rights of the peasants to choose between retaining their land and handing it over to the government for a compensation.
11. Once a bourgeois legal right to forest resources is documented, this becomes saleable, creating the potential for concentration of ownership. As long as the possession of these resources vested with the community in the form of traditionally recognised rights, not documented in a bourgeois legal sense, these were not saleable.
12. Burial by water.

6

The World Trade Organisation: The Police of Global Capital

Preliminaries

It is a major contention of this book that there is no predetermined path of capitalist development. So its rules cannot be uncovered by any logical exercise. It is not even as if there is a pure capitalist path, charted in the West, and a corrupt or semi-feudal path, followed in the colonies or neo-colonies like India. A part of the profit appropriated by capital is actually capitalist rent whose quantum and distribution among the appropriating classes are decided by forcible creation and occupation of private rights whether it be over natural resources, stock of knowledge, or over markets. We have also discussed another significance of the existence of such rent. Capital sucks surplus produced within non-capitalist enterprise in the form of capitalist rent. So there is no inviolable rule that the further the boundaries of territories dominated by capital extend, the greater will be the proportion of production within capitalist enterprise. In fact, the current trend is to fragment mammoth capitalist enterprises, putting out parts of the production process, often to non-capitalist enterprise. The name commonly used nowadays to designate such activity is Business Process Outsourcing (BPO), and the enterprises are called BPO firms. The non-capitalist sector also sustains and expands global capital's claim to surplus in another way, as we have discussed in the context of the significance of rent extraction by global capital. The refugees of development crowd the fringes of the urban agglomerations as the new outcasts. They provide a number of support services to the organised sector workers. This allows the capitalist enterprises in the organised sector to pay lower wages and salaries to their employees than would otherwise have been possible. Thus the surplus produced by the marginalised also bloats the profits of global capital as a species of rent.

There is no unique path of capitalist development. Neither do the refugees of capitalist growth have a definite identity. These refugees of modern development, who have been robbed of ancient common rights over land, forests and water resources, form new communities of outcasts or the marginalised, submitting to the rule of global capital. They are resigned to their new position as subjects of global capital but try to limit or modify the kingly ethics with their, the subjects', plea for life. The globally revered priests of development economics represent their case in the courts of global capital. The evolved, tempered kingly ethics and the commitment of King Capital to such ethics finds expression in the welfarist policies of World Bank.

The World Trade Organisation (WTO), on the other hand, functions as the enforcement agency, the economic police of the new world, maintaining the appropriate order in the territories colonised by global capital. The objectives of this institution are much more transparent than that of the World Bank. The task of WTO (and its predecessor, General Agreement on Trade and Tariff - GATT) is (was) quite straightforward: to ensure the mobility of commodities and capital to the extent desired by global capital. As long as capital bore national tags, GATT used to work mainly in the interest of US capital. With the advance of globalisation, GATT and more clearly WTO have been functioning at the behest of global capital. These organisations have never bothered to mask their objectives. Their principal activity has been to force member countries to modify and, if necessary, to completely change their tax, tariff, and subsidy policies, as well as laws relating to property in the interest of whichever capital is globally dominant at that time. By stretching the boundaries of the territory dominated by global capital, they have facilitated and continue to facilitate rent extraction. They spearhead global capital's economic campaign to possess natural resources, stock of knowledge and markets.

The Beginning

The foundation of GATT/WTO was laid after the Second World War at the time when the IMF and World Bank were created. After some international parleys and negotiations, the UNO convened a conference at Havana in 1948. The Havana Charter, the outcome of this conference, contained a plan to set up an International Trade Organisation (ITO) that would have the power to intervene in the policies of member countries relating to international trade, tariff and even employment and economic development. The US Senate, however, refused to ratify the Charter on the ground that this would curb the economic sovereignty of America. Actually the Senate opposed the formation of the ITO because it was proposed that the organisation would be under the control of the UNO. It was feared that the USA might not always be able to control and fine-tune the decisions of the UNO. In this context, it should be mentioned that the UNO has no control over WTO. Other countries abandoned the plan for ITO because they felt that it would be ineffective if the richest nation did not join it. As a result GATT, which was based on the provisional agreement on trade and tariff that was reached in the run-up to the Havana Charter, became the guideline for international trade regulation.

GATT

The main objective of GATT was to free international trade from the controls exercised by national governments. Various arguments have been advanced since the eighteenth century for and against free trade. In practice, a country that is technologically advanced, would, naturally desire free trade. At one time Britain advocated free trade (though she continued to impose tariffs at high rates on imports of manufactures from

India). Later when she had lost her supremacy over the industrial world, she leaned towards protectionist policies. Just after the Second World War, the USA was the most advanced country in terms of financial and technological strength. So it was in her interest to propagate free trade. But there are also other advantages of being powerful. Britain had violated her professed policy and imposed high tariffs on imports of manufactures from India. Similarly, the USA succeeded in keeping out of the general framework of GATT, all sectors in which free trade would have impeded her national interest.

GATT gave effect to its basic objectives through three principles: the principle of liberalisation, the principle of reciprocity, and the principle of Most Favoured Nation (MFN). The principle of liberalisation involved reduction in tariff and non-tariff barriers to the international mobility of goods. The principle of reciprocity required that if a member reduced its tariffs, its trading partners had to follow suit. The MFN principle states that each member must treat all other members as MFN. That is, if a member extended some privileges with respect to trade (e.g. reduction in tariff, increase in quota) to any member, it had to extend the same facilities to every other member of GATT.

During the life-span of GATT, eight Multilateral Trade Negotiations (MTNs) were held to decide on ways to put into effect the desired goals of GATT. At every MTN, the number of participating countries increased, tariff rates were reduced on a large number of commodities, and at each successive MTN the rate of reduction of rate of tariff increased. The poor countries began participating in these MTNs in greater numbers since the seventh MTN (1973–1979). Till this MTN, the work of GATT had been limited to reduction of restrictions on trade between the rich countries. But gradually the focus of GATT began to shift towards trade between rich and poor countries. The poor countries had expected that as a result of intervention by GATT the discrimination practised by the rich countries against the poor ones in international trade would be reduced. Events belied and in fact diametrically opposed these expectations. This was but natural. If one examines the exemptions that were made by

GATT, either in the way of keeping some sectors totally out of the purview of GATT, or by way of accommodation under special arrangements, it becomes quite clear whose interest GATT was serving.

Exemptions

It was claimed that GATT would work towards reduction of intervention by governments in international trade and, particularly, towards reduction in protective tariff. But at its very inception it was decided that trade in agricultural commodities would be kept out of the purview of GATT. Europe and the USA easily came to an understanding on this issue because both subsidised their agricultural sector heavily. If the market for agricultural products had not been protected at that point of time, domestic agricultural production would have altogether ceased in these countries, or such a high rate of subsidy would have had to be paid that the government would not have been able to absorb the pressure.

For similar reasons, the cotton-weaving sector was kept out of the GATT. From the 1960s the textile industry of Western Europe began to face stiff competition from the exports of Japan and some underdeveloped countries. The European nations could have invoked special clauses of the GATT to protect their textile industry, but in that case they would have to limit the trade in textiles among themselves also. As a preferred option they forced GATT to approve a special regime for trade in textiles. First, a so-called Short Term Agreement on textiles was adopted. Then successively, a Long-Term Agreement, a Multi Fibre Agreement and ultimately an Agreement on Textiles and Clothing were forced on GATT/WTO by the rich nations. The basic approach of all these agreements was the same: there would be a fixed limit on the exports of the underdeveloped countries to the developed countries. The duplicity practised by the rich countries is quite clearly seen in Clause 6.1 of the Multi Fibre Agreement (MFA). It is mentioned in this clause that in fixing these limits, the underdeveloped countries would be given some advantage, while the entire purpose of the agreement was to reduce the exports of the underdeveloped countries to the developed countries.

We can cite such examples ad infinitum. All the examples would only emphasise the same basic fact. However much the priests of open markets may chant praises of free markets, markets are freed wherever and to whatever extent it suits the interests of those segments of capital, which are powerful in the international economic arena. In the age of globalisation, this proposition has to be modified to fit the changed circumstances. We will discuss the necessary changes at a later point.

The Uruguay Round

The last round of MTN was held in Uruguay from 1986 to 1994. This round marked the end of an era. The curtain formally dropped on the age of capitalism where each capital had a national label. The legal framework and the monitoring agency that are necessary to facilitate the smooth mobility of commodities and capital to the extent desired by global capital began to be put in place from this round of MTN. The preparatory work was completed, with the formation of WTO in 1995.

Decisions that were qualitatively different were taken with respect to areas that were already under the purview of GATT. Also, new areas were brought under GATT, and later under WTO.

The quantity of textiles that could be exported by third world countries was fixed by the Agreement on Textiles and Clothing. It was also promised that over a span of ten years, quotas on textile exports would be totally removed. An agreement was also reached to abolish all subsidies on textile exports by a specific date.

Besides this, new areas were brought under the scope of GATT/WTO. The most significant were the trade in services, intellectual properties and international investment.

Services were brought under GATT through the General Agreement on Trade in Services (GATS). All the rules and regulations, which governed the trade in goods, were extended to the trade in services through GATS. All member nations were forced to adopt a universal set of laws relating to intellectual properties through the Agreement on Trade-related Aspects of Intellectual Properties (TRIPS). The objective of Agreement on Trade-related Aspects of Investment Measures (TRIMS) was to terminate all laws relating to foreign investment, which were intended to curb their inflow. For example, it could no longer be made mandatory that enterprises where foreign investment was allowed would have to export a certain proportion of their output. The argument advanced was that such clauses were anathema to the very principles of GATT/WTO because they limited imports of capital. Though TRIMS was formally non-discriminatory, the fact is that it was clearly meant to prevent some developing countries, including India, from curbing the inflow of foreign capital or channelising it in directions that were acceptable to their planners.

The Significance of Changes

It is not within the scope of this study to discuss all the merits and demerits of the various novel measures adopted at the Uruguay round of MTN. There is a vast literature on this issue, which is a must for all those wishing to seriously understand the new economic order.[1] Here, we will just highlight the novelty of the measures with the help of some examples. As those readers who have followed through our arguments can easily anticipate, a particular critical attitude will inform our analysis of the originality of these agreements, that is, of the way in which these differ from those reached in the previous rounds of MTNs. But, to labour a point, no analysis in social science is unbiased, no matter what be its public posture: our critical attitude also obliquely refers to a positive position, which we will elaborate upon in our concluding chapter.

The service sector had been excluded from the jurisdiction of GATT because it was felt that the resultant interference in the sovereign legal process of the country was not desirable. To export services it is necessary that the service-providing agency belonging to the exporting nation must be physically present within the territory of the importing nation. This is because service is a commodity whose production and sale cannot be separated. Shoes are produced in factories, for instance, and may be stocked at retail outlets for future sale to users. But insurance, banking and transport cannot be stocked for future sale. Hence the production and sale of insurance occurs at the same spot. Allowing the import of services, therefore, implies foreign direct investment in the service sector. Not only that, branches of foreign service-providers are partially staffed with foreign employees and managers. Since foreign investment was outside the scope of GATT, prior to the Uruguay Round of MTN, trade in services had also to be excluded. It was also argued that if foreign service-providers were allowed to set up their subsidiaries, then the government of the service importer would lose some of its sovereign right to decide who could enter or stay in the country, as foreign nationals would be employed in the subsidiaries and branches. Following the Uruguay Round, trade in services has been brought under the purview of GATT (through GATS) and later WTO, but trade in labour service remains the lone exemption. Though sale of labour services is just another kind of service transaction, it was excluded from the purview of GATS. So the unemployed from our country cannot enter the USA in search of jobs, though a US corporation is free to enter our country in search of insurance markets.

The lack of interest in incorporating foreign investment within the scope of GATT, at the time of its inception, can be explained partly by the ruling orthodoxy in theory relating to economic policy at that time. The dominant belief was that in order to solve the basic economic problems of a country, the government should adopt suitable fiscal and monetary policies for expansion or contraction of aggregate demand. This was the basic contention of Keynesian economics. But if there is free mobility of foreign capital, the effectiveness of such policy declines appreciably. Suppose that, for whatever reason, the government wants to reduce the rate of investment. It is widely believed that if the rate of interest increases then the rate of investment falls. One simple reason for this dependence is that interest is the cost of funds, which are invested.[2] So, in order to decrease the rate of investment, the government increases the rate of interest. If foreign capital inflow were unchecked, the higher rate of interest would attract more foreign capital and so defeat the government's objective. This would constitute sufficient reason for excluding foreign investment from the scope of GATT if one believes that policy is determined by 'scientific', economic theory. In fact, however, the dominant economic theory of a time and the dominant economic interests of the time are mutually constitutive. When GATT was established, capital was identifiable by nationality. Contradiction between American capital and British capital, for instance, was significant. So national capital insisted that it should have the leverage to control domestic economic policy within the national boundary. This leverage would have been curbed, to an extent, if foreign capital had been given total freedom of entry.

Times have changed. This is the age of globalisation. That is, in many ways capital now lacks a national identity. Globalised capital wants to cross international boundaries going to and fro without hindrance. Hence the current interest in using international economic agencies like the WTO to gain international access to investment fields. This explains the interest in measures like TRIMS and GATS. The fact that the right to free mobility of labour failed to gain recognition while the free mobility of other services has been put on the cards is generally seen as a failure of the poor nations to push their point of view at international forums. Such broad generalisations are not at all fruitful. Except perhaps in a wartime situation, when national chauvinism becomes the dominant national ethos, it is misleading to interpret events in terms of conflicts between nations. It would be advantageous to labour if free mobility of labour services is permitted, but it is certainly against the interests of large 'Indian capital' (that is globalised), which profits from the maintenance of pockets of misery in the 'third world'. Such capital is interested in using this vast hinterland of poverty to extract rent in various ways, which we have already discussed. In this respect at least, there is no difference between the objectives of such capital and so-called 'foreign capital'. It is pointless to treat the nation as one entity except, perhaps, when nationalism', 'patriotism' and such other sentiments become the principal guiding force for large segments of the population. In normal times, as a result of pulls and pushes of economic interests there are contradictions, as well as collaboration and compromise between nations. In such compromises, which nation takes the subservient position, to what extent, what will be the quality of such compromise; what will be the altered nature of national identity under the changed circumstances – these are the questions to which we must seek answers in order to build towards a theory of contemporary imperialism. This is a huge task. No one can fill the gigantic canvas by lone effort. Various studies dealing with diverse single aspects of the economy have to intercourse to symbiotically generate a picture of the totality. But each little effort has to be informed with the theoretical perception that reality is overdetermined, that is all the partial aspects mutually constitute one another. Further, the reality of the dominated part of the global economy and that of the dominating or imperial aspect are also interdependent, though there is a hierarchy involved in this process. There is an asymmetry in the process of mutual determination.[3] For instance, global capital forces a uniform structure of laws and development process which marginalises forest dependent people, they are forced into marginal forms of employment where the surplus they produce is siphoned off as rent which is unrecorded, passing off as profit of global capital. This surplus then is a determinant of the rate of growth of global capital.

The rules and regulations of GATT/WTO have been extended to trade in services. The official rules and restraints pertaining to trade in these commodities have been freed from protectionism. But the mobility of labour has not been ensured. Who stands to gain from such double standards? Obviously the capital that is free to move all over the globe to take advantage of the low wage areas that are preserved as a result of the immobility of labour, that is global capital. Poor countries are plagued with a chronic unemployment problem. Moreover, the market cost of the desired standard of living of labour in these countries is lower. All told, wages are lower in the poor countries. If the labourers could freely migrate to the rich countries, the intensity of the unemployment problem would have declined in the poor countries. Wages would have increased as a result. The rate of profit on capital invested in these countries would have decreased. But how would this adversely affect capital in the rich countries? They should rather gain as the influx of labour to these countries depresses wages. In the current context, however, the result is likely to be the opposite. One must remember that large capital has no nationality today. Besides, one must also bear in mind that the current tendency is towards fragmentation of integrated production processes, coupled with putting out of parts of the processes even to destinations outside the countries in which the original factory is located. Because wages are low in the poor countries, enterprises in the advanced capitalist countries can put out work to firms located in these countries to earn greater profits. We have suggested that modern technology hastens this process. Editing, composing, proof reading for Oxford University Press, for example, is done by some firms located in poor countries. So, in the changed circumstances, global capital (it is really pointless talking about the nationality of capital) has vested interest in keeping labour tied down within the national boundaries. As long as capital was predominantly bounded within a nation, it made sense to force the nation to adopt policies that would lower the level of wages lower within the nation state. But with globalisation, large capital is no longer interested in keeping wages low in a particular country. It is rather interested in enforcing such policies that lead to the preservation of low-wage enclaves in the poor countries. They can use the depressed condition in these locations in two ways. They can fragment the production processes in the parent company, now controlled by global capital, and put out parts of the processes to the poor territories; or they can use the poverty to directly invest to take advantage of the low wages and poverty. We mention the fact of poverty separately because this itself sustains the low-wage economy. The marginalised population, mainly made up of the refugees of development, provides various support services to the wageworkers employed both in the BPO enterprises as well as in the MNCs themselves. Such services include housekeeping, laundry, and various odd jobs. As a result, wages in the organised sector in poor countries can be maintained at levels which are much lower than that paid to their counterparts in the developed countries.

Because of a lack of foresight, labour located in the rich countries suffers from the illusion that the limitations on the immigration of labour from the poor countries works in their interest, as immigration would have lowered their own wages. They have not been able to grasp the fact that what passes as globalisation, today, is also globalisation of poverty. One way or the other, the working people in the rich countries, who had reaped the benefit of belonging to an imperial centre as long as capital had a national identity, are no longer immunised from the dismal fate of their poor counterpart in the 'third world'. Labour is prohibited entry to the rich nations (not as a concession to labour in those countries, but at the behest of global capital) but jobs are exported. The working class in the advanced countries cannot insulate itself. But labour in the rich countries still labours under the illusion that it can shield itself from the poverty in other parts of the world. National chauvinism adds another dimension to this purely economic illusion. At the same time, chauvinism gets a new content and expression. Globalised capital takes advantage of the labour's shortsightedness to enforce policies that ensure the preservation and expansion of pockets of abject poverty. It then uses these to reap rent disguised as profit.

GATS and TRIMS were necessary in order to bring about the changes in the structure of economic policies, which are consistent with the evolution of nationally divided capital into global capital. TRIPS too is connected with this change but its area of operation and objective are different. Global capital can sanctify and enforce its occupation of rights over land, water, forests, and mineral resources and even over local stock of knowledge through the promulgation of uniform patent laws. So its power of rent extraction increases. Through GATS and TRIMS and the creation of WTO, the control of global capital over markets is strengthened. So, rent as supernormal profit can be extracted with greater impunity. On the other hand,

TRIPS helps strengthen the hold over resources which capital acquires from outside its organisational preserve. This right allows global capital to extract rent from the deployment of such resources. The need for TRIPS points to a fundamental character of global capital in this era, which we have already elaborated upon – the increasing dependence of global capital on rent extraction. Further, as rent extraction depends on the establishment of rights that allow extraction of rent, TRIPS depends positively on the powers of the state. To highlight the special significance of TRIPS compared to measures like TRIMS or GATS, one can suggest that while the latter two are dependent on the state in a negative way, the former depends positively on the application of the powers of the state. That is, in a sense TRIMS and GATS depend on the abrogation of what used to be the restrictive powers of the state, while TRIPS requires the state to promulgate and enforce new laws and regulations enshrining new laws of property. TRIPS even contains new concepts of jurisprudence: if a party is alleged to have violated certain patent laws like, say, the Plant Breeder Rights, then the party will be held to be guilty unless proved innocent. This violates our entire concept of legal truth where a party is held to be innocent unless proved guilty.

NOTES

1. Interested readers may contact the following organisations for literature on the impact of the measures adopted by WTO on poor countries (with special reference to India): National Working Group on Patent Laws, A-388, Sarita Vihar, New Delhi 110044. entre for Study of Global Trade System and Development, A-388 Sarita Vihar, New Delhi.
2. Interest is directly paid if the funds are borrowed. If own funds are invested, then interest is the cost in the sense that it is the income sacrificed by not lending out the accumulated funds.
3. This has been termed 'mimicry of overdetermination'. We have referred to this idea on page 4.

7

The New Strategy of Global Capital

The international economic order that has come into being as a result of the pervasive intervention of the IMF, World Bank and WTO and, in the event that this proves ineffective, the military campaigns led by US Marines, has two significant characteristics. First, its rules, regulations and mechanism of settlement of international disputes are such that the worldwide mobility of capital is becoming ever smoother. Second, global capital is able to reap rent disguised as profit by restricting the mobility of labour, local small sector's output, knowledge, science and information technology.

Rent is extracted by restricting the spatial mobility of products and inputs. Land and natural resources are intrinsically immobile. So, it is possible to extract rent from the use of these resources by establishing rights over defined geographical territories. This process has been at work since the birth of capital. The only novelty in the age of globalisation is that the national laws pertaining to the ownership of land and land-based resources are being are being altered so that global capital can acquire such rights, just as any citizen of the country. Previously this was not legally possible. Introduction of contract farming, relaxation of ceiling on the size of land holding are all indicators of this process.

In the age of globalisation, resources that are not intrinsically immobile are also rendered immobile through various legal, political and technological processes in order to facilitate rent extraction by global capital. Just as international rules and regulations are being used towards this end, appropriate technology is also being evolved.

Free Mobility of Capital/Immobility of Inputs

Let us try to understand the propositions with the help of some examples. In a recent book, Chakraborty and Cullenberg (Chakraborty, A. and Cullenberg, S., 2003) have tried to understand the predicament of the small-scale sector in India in the context of liberalisation. They have shown how the WTO restricts the export of the output of this sector on the ground that this sector violates international environmental and labour standards. It is not as if production is stopped at the behest of these organisations, because these standards have been violated. The small-scale sector may produce at low cost by employing child labour, by engaging workforce on inhuman terms, by polluting the environment. The small-scale readymade garment-manufacturing industry in south India supplying garments for such international brands as Nike and Adidas is just one of the many such segments of industry. There is no bar on that. Such products will be purchased by global capital to be used as intermediate products or to be marketed with their brand labels. That is, the product market is being restricted and bounded. Only global capital has the visas for crossing these boundaries. The rest can enter only after being branded as the property of global capital. Global capital extracts rent from the monopoly of rights of entry. The small-scale sector, for instance, produces at low cost because it employs labour at low cost and ignores environmental norms. Enterprises owned by global capital buy such products and sell them at their cost of production under competitive conditions. The difference is appropriated as rent disguised as profit. The BPO story is much the same. Global capital has monopoly control over the market for final goods and services. Some of the intermediate stages of production are put out to call centres and such enterprises located in poor countries. If the employees of call centres could enter the rich countries freely, they could seek employment at much greater wages. Mobility of labour is curbed in order to take advantage of the low wages in the poor countries, which is the result of the unemployment problem in these countries. To reap the benefits of low wages, work is put out to enterprises in the poor countries. Thus, taking advantage of the resulting low overall cost of production, global capital earns rent which is disguised as supernormal profit. By using this strategy, global capital is reaping huge rents from the healthcare business, publishing, marketing of different commodities, etc.

The new laws pertaining to intellectual properties (TRIPS) formulated by GATT/WTO have opened unexplored vistas for rent extraction by global capital. Patenting is now possible in areas like plant varieties, uses of plant varieties, etc. which were previously off limits, at least in India. Permission has to be obtained from a patentee for use of the patented product or resource (tangible or intangible). This is granted on payment or royalty, which is a form of rent. Predictably, folk knowledge, knowledge of plant varieties which were traditionally possessed by the poor forest dwellers will be appropriated by global capital using their money power and their experience in 'scientific documentation' of discoveries. Common knowledge and forest resources will cease to be part of the tribal or community heritage. Traditional channels of knowledge communication will be cut off. Thus, by restricting the free flow of knowledge and natural transmission of plant varieties, new areas are being created for rent extraction. One can try to minimise the theft of such knowledges by global capital by making plant and gene registers. This is being done in many regions like Kerala and Maharashtra. But the point is that the new laws and regulations convert community or common property into private property that is suitable for exchange within the market. Sooner or later there must be a concentration of such property, as of all property, thus enhancing the rent-earning ability of large capital, which in today's context is global capital.

The path of evolution of technology is never decided by so-called scientific reasoning alone. Like other processes, this too is determined by the play of many interests. From a class focus it appears that the direction of technological evolution in the age of globalisation is determined by the need of global capital to extract rent. Some researchers are currently analysing how Microsoft is doing exactly this in the field of software technology.[1] Grossly, one can put it thus: innumerable PC users use Windows Programmes mechanically. They remain ignorant of the specifics of computer technology, of its potential. They cannot differentiate between a Windows operating system and computers. As a result, Microsoft has a stranglehold on the market for operating systems and programmes for PCs. To perpetuate this hold, the operating systems technology is evolving in such a way that the programmes that are being written into it remain obscure to the user. A laziness of mind, an uncritical use of tool-bags (whether cultural or technological) always works in the service of the existing distribution of power. Evolution of so-called user-friendly programmes by Microsoft Windows, therefore, increases the dependence of PC users on Microsoft and so works in the service of maintaining the stranglehold of Microsoft Corp. on the software market.

Genetic engineering is also being used for rent extraction. I feel that the progress in this field is inextricably linked to the economics of monopoly control over markets and of rent extraction. It is not possible to use patent laws to establish ownership over natural gene varieties, which are in wide use. One can claim ownership only by establishing human input in the form of genetic engineering. But, realistically, it is not possible to enforce ownership over engineered varieties unless their natural reproduction can be blocked.[2] So the biological structure of seeds is being so modified that natural reproduction of seeds does not occur. Seeds cannot be derived from crops. Farmers become dependent on global capital for this basic input. So Cargill and Monsanto can extract rent almost at will. New technology is therefore evolving in a way so as to block the natural and free transmission of seeds, to block natural reproduction. A new field for rent extraction by global capital is being fenced off by the technologically imposed barrier to free transfer of this essential agricultural input through natural reproduction.

In sum, the claim that globalisation means free mobility of goods, services, capital and resources across the globe is a motivated fiction. Globalisation of course means unfettered movement of multinational monopoly capital. But it is also the process of restricting the flow of working people, information technology, knowledge and science and even that of the natural capacity of reproduction. By appropriating proprietary rights over these segmented spaces or by establishing control over such spaces through monopoly over markets, global capital extracts rent. Globalisation simply means the aggressive occupation of various kinds of spaces by global capital in order to extract rent. This process can also be designated as primitive capital accumulation of the new age.

State Power in the New Age

Who is the subject of this manoeuvre? Does capital not have any national identity? If it does not have such identity, then what explains the conflict between the rich and poor nations at international economic forums? And, what is perhaps the most significant question: What is imperialism in this age of global capital?

We find no ground to subscribe to a theory of withering away of states in this 'higher' stage of world capitalism, though this has gained some following even among the left intelligentsia. We have argued that the basic thrust of all policy initiatives in this period is towards curtailing the economic sovereignty of poor nations. The poor countries do not give up their sovereignty voluntarily, either. There is a well-orchestrated campaign to force these nations to accept such a policy framework. The international economic organisations are the principal organisers of the economic component of this campaign. Of course, if the need arises, global capital is not shy of using the military muscle of the US Marines and their sidekicks to make the recalcitrant nations toe the line. How does one reconcile the apparent inconsistency between what we have designated as the globalisation of capital and the intensification of pressure on some nations (i.e. the poor nations) to achieve some specific economic goals?

Global capital does not have any geographical identity. In fact, one cannot even say that it is primarily centred in the rich nations. In its sourcing and in the spread of the locations of its investment, it is truly global. Examples abound of Indian firms buying up competing or collaborating firms in the developed countries. (And what ecstasy we, the articulate standard bearers of the nation, show when Tata takes over Corus Steel!). In spite of this, there is a strong dependence of global capital on the governments of the rich nations for reasons that we shall presently discuss. From this angle, to propound the theory that in this age of global capital the states are withering away is to, wittingly or unwittingly, play into the hands of global capital.

The campaign launched by global capital to obtain control over various spaces, or to obtain superior rights over these spaces, is essentially the process of PCA, which is unceasing. PCA needs the support of ruling authority. Therefore, it needs a defined seat of power. If rights were really and truly undifferentiated then the state could, perhaps, be the mythical expression of a common will that the bourgeois state is touted to be. But the capitalist order, like any 'order', is inherently hierarchical, contrary to its mythological representation. Superior rights over segmented spaces together with immobility for some is the source of capitalist rent. There used to be common rights or traditional community rights over resources like knowledge and science, plant varieties, etc. These rights were uprooted and supplanted with unconditional, sole individual or institutional rights of the capitalist order.

The notion of global governance has gained currency in political science. If capital be globalised and if its interests be the principle motive force behind the current phase of history, then the world should be moving towards uniform laws and administrative regulations, which implies unified governance. This, in a particular way, amounts to withering away of the nation states. Though our focus does not allow sufficient space for a critique of this idea, we would still venture that this is a rather hollow theory. Without going deeply into the ethico-political and philosophical questions involved, we can observe that nation states can wither only when a sense of universal humanism pervades the globe - when, through ceaseless criticism and self-criticism, this sense becomes socially manifest, (that is it manifests itself in the cessation of exploitation and hierarchy at every level) and is strengthened and internalised by humanity at large.

PCA is based on territorial occupation. The presence of capitalist rent reveals a deep fissure in what appears otherwise to be an unbroken surface of capitalist order, constructed on strictly rational principles. It indicates the unavoidable hierarchy, which is a necessary constituent of the system. The structure of unequal rights cannot be justified by rational principles. It cannot be the result of any process of argument and conclusion, that is a dialectical process. At its base lies coercion, plain and simple. Who should be entitled to the right over an invention, over a segment of knowledge? Should such rights be recognised at all? These are questions to which there cannot be any logical answer. Such are decided only by force. WTO is attempting to impose a specific uniform set of rules regarding intellectual properties on all nations to facilitate rent extraction by global capital. The first world countries under the leadership of the USA, are trying to rigorously impose these rules and regulations all over the world. At the same time, the technology pirates are waging a kind of guerrilla war against this campaign by copying the technologies owned by global capital or the products of such technologies. The governments of nations where large productive sectors are based on such 'piracy' extend covert help to such 'pirates'. Where there is no uniformity of logic, a tussle of strength is inevitable. And strength or power needs a bearer. So, to states, and to conflict between states. All this talk of global governance is part of the mythology of the ruling order, sustained by its illusions, which is proving to be a happy hunting ground for globalised researchers.

Where logic fails (as post-modernism[3] claims it always must), force stops the gaps. Force must have an agency. Thus far there is not much that will generate acute disagreement. But why must power of the nation state necessarily be this agency? Obviously, global capital will try to realise the full potential of rent extraction on the basis of the new level of PCA, in this age of global capitalism. In order to appropriate rent from newer domains, global capital must have control over the legal and administrative machinery of the geographical territories in which these domains are located. Power over a geographical region is state power. But is it not possible for such power itself to be globalised? This is not conceivable because there is no general, inevitable, logical basis of property rights. Laws and administration are all props to support a specific set of property rights. Global capital is bent on imposing on all nations a basic set of laws and an administrative set-up using the state power of the rich nations and the power of economic coercion of the international economic organisations. Other economic interest groups or classes, some of which are still locally powerful, stand to gain from the prevailing local laws and administrative system. They, naturally oppose attempts to revamp the system. Conflicts result. So, global capital can ensure a solution, which suits it only through coercive measures. It is not as if global capital has any hang-ups about some 'pure' set of laws and regulations which it willy-nilly imposes. Such purity exists only in the mind of intellectuals drugged by the opulence of global markets. Coercion is not the instrument of choice for any ruler. Global capital, therefore, tries to install the economic regime that it requires following a path of least resistance. Towards this end, it reaches various kinds of adjustments with local powers. Thus, there emerge many variations of the basic economic system, which are perfectly suitable to global capital. There is, therefore, no reason for the emergence of global governance.

Contradiction and Over-determination

The driving force of the current phase of world economic history is global capital. However, it is the nation states of different countries, which have unleashed a frenzy of primitive capital accumulation for the benefit of global capital. At first sight this may appear to be paradoxical. But the notion of over-determination in contradiction, supplemented with the notion of hierarchy is one way of reconciling with the apparent inconsistency.

We will try to explain this supplemented notion by analogy

with a familiar situation. To maintain its legislative authority and its sphere of influence, a political party often uses goons. We are more or less familiar with the activities of these dons. The dons have their own positions to protect. So, the parties in power have to compromise with them on various issues. The powerful dons retain various smaller hoods. They exert pressure on their respective dons to demand this or that favour from the political authority. But if the demands of a don become too extravagant, the political authority revokes the territorial lease given to that don and awards the lease to another don. How far a don will be pampered or how capable a political party is of revoking the lease given to a particular don depends on the strength of the don. The more powerful a don, the more the dependence on the don and more demands the political authority is willing to concede. Naturally, in this case the don can accommodate more demands from the underlings. The political authority, don and underlings together constitute an overdetermined totality within which there is hierarchy – political authority is at the top, the don just below and the small-time goons at the lowest level. One can find parallels to the main characters involved in the play of globalisation within this portrayal of the political-underworld nexus. The party in power or political authority represents global capital. The big, powerful dons stand for the governments of rich countries. The weaker dons can stand for the governments of the poorer nations. The underlings of the dons can be identified with the powerful forces within a nation.

Pressure and Compromise

Global capital depends on the state power of the rich nations at two levels – economic and political. Global capital cannot directly plead its own demands at international economic organisations because these are not class-based but nation-based institutions. Global capital's case is argued by the rich nations. There is logic behind global capital's lack of interest in imposing its order directly. To defend power, the instrument of choice is persuasion, not coercion. There is nothing like it, if the exploited are willing to be exploited. Bringing classes to the fore, therefore, is not wise. The textbooks of International Trade disseminate this myth in a crude way: their models talk exclusively of nations as independent decision-making units. The use of nations as the primary categories instead of exposing the class interests, probably works in the service of defusing class tensions or in preventing them from surfacing.

The international economic organisations are not the only armies of economic warfare that global capital has at its command to enforce laws and regulations that serve its interests all over the world. If any decision of WTO does not favour global capital or if there is lack of clarity (which is wilfully retained) in some clause, rich nations, at the behest of global capital, force poor nations through bilateral 'negotiations' to accept 'voluntarily' clauses, which more definitely favour global capital. WTO recognises the legality of such voluntary surrenders, in order to keep this option open to global capital. Global capital does not depend on rich nations in order to exert economic pressure alone. If some nation refuses to fall in line in spite of so much pressure, global capital has to fall back on the time-tested instrument of imperial expansion – outright warfare. For this it has to rely on the armies of the rich nations led by the USA.

Because of its manifold dependence on the governments of rich nations, global capital has to grant concessions to them in much the same manner that political authority has to often pander to the big dons. True, these governments predominantly look after the interests of global capital. But, in order to maintain their own power base, these governments have to accommodate some demands of other powerful and organised forces. The farmers' lobby in these countries is one particularly striking example. Because of the pressure exerted by this lobby, it is not possible to completely abolish agricultural subsidies or to completely liberalise the trade in agricultural commodities. The WTO also has to legalise such exemptions under pressure from the governments of the rich countries.

Global Capital versus the Poor

Global capital has conflict of interest with various economic groups in the poor countries. There is antagonism in the conflicts or contradictions between the interests of global capital and that of the vast majority of the population in the poor countries. It is not possible to reach any compromise between the interests of global capital and those of this segment of the population. Given the dominance of global capital, the governments of these countries do not have the liberty to accede to the demands of this poor majority. Their pleas for food and shelter do not enter the calculations of their states. This abjectly poor mass either finds employment on the fringes of the economic system or simply lives outside the system, as unemployed. The fundamental structural changes that are necessary to fulfill the basic human needs of this mass would cause a transformation in the character of state power. Crumbs of relief are earmarked for these fringe dwellers. Even such crumbs are becoming few and far between as the cultural dominance of the morality of the market place is increasing. The poverty-stricken 'citizen' too has no expectation from the state. By now they have more or less seen through the bluff of citizenship. They enter only one book of accounts of the state – the record of law and order. They have no reason to accept the rules and regulations of the existing socio-economic system, to internalise its order. It is but natural that what appears ethical to them should appear unethical to the established order and so be branded as illegal.

One of the segments with which global capital has a relation of conflict is that of the workers in capitalist enterprise. We have argued that that the predominant mode of operation of global capital is to fence off territories (not just geographical), restrict mobility across the boundaries and, using these restrictions extract rent. The restrictions imposed on international mobility of labour provide an example of how the system works.[4] Global capital can gain from this segmentation only if minimum wages, maximum hours of work and such are not fixed by law. Governments of poor countries have been aggressively curbing trade union rights during the globalisation period because floor on wages, ceiling on hours worked are part of the basic agenda of all trade unions. Generally, the trade unions in the poor countries do not pose much of a problem. In our country the trade unions function as appendages of political parties. These parties, in spite of their much-trumpeted ideological differences, are all quite smitten by the marketplace. Or, because of the lack of a vision of an alternative path, they have prostrated themselves before the God of the Market. Recently, the chief minister of a state ruled for thirty long years by a left alliance has declared that the alliance is bent on pursuing the capitalist path of development, with all the pomp of lifting the veil shrouding a closely guarded state secret! The same chief minister (whom one should credit with lack of prevarication) argued that the IT industry should be treated as an essential sector and exempted from the purview of strikes called by the trade unions – this to maintain their national and international competitiveness. Significantly, his party did not demur either.

Global Capital versus National Capital

There are some interest groups within the poor countries who have the muscle to make their respective governments take some action in their favour, though this may conflict with the interests of global capital. Within these segments, perhaps, the group most difficult to accommodate within our theoretical frame is what is called 'national capital'. This fraction of capital has received much attention within leftist political and academic discourse ever since the idea of New Democracy[5] gained currency. Once upon a not-so-distant past, it used to be argued in these circles that the greatest enemies of the nation were the imperialist forces and their underlings, the collaborating or comprador capitalists within the country and the remnants of the feudal landed aristocracy. The need of the hour was to form a national alliance against them. Together with other classes and groups, national capital also had to be roped into this alliance. Through the 1960s and the 1970s, there used to be stormy debates about whether capital was predominantly national or predominantly collaborator in nature; which segment was nationalist and which segment was collaborator. At that time capital had definite national tags, or so it used to be believed. As the mobility of capital has increased, its identity has tended to become blurred. US enterprises are being bought by Korean capital. Indian capital is purchasing British and

American enterprises. We are simply reiterating a well-documented phenomenon: imperial capital is no longer geocentric. Big capital is global. If it is not actually, in potential it definitely is. The additional insight, which comes through in the course of our analysis, is that global capital is a belligerent force, aggressively occupying existing or newly defined spaces for appropriating rent. It is inherently imperialist quite in the old sense. There is unity among the different fractions of global capital though there is, obviously, competition among them. There is unity in keeping local capital (which is small capital) confined territorially in order to be able to extract greater amount of rent. If one does not look analytically at these phenomena, one is quite likely to think that the two aspects (collaboration and competition) are of the same order. Even the respective governments may sometimes play a part in the competitive friction. Whether or not a government will get involved depends on factors like intensity of the conflict, the quantitative significance of the conflict to the national economy and the dependence of the government on the fractions involved in the conflict. One may even confuse the aggressive postures the governments sometimes adopt in such cases as expressions of anti-imperialist commitment of the government. A case in point was the opposition of France to the American occupation of Iraq. France was seen by many as a born-again champion of those oppressed by imperialism, while in fact the government was simply trying to ensure that the USA did not unduly benefit from its occupation of Iraq. It was opposed to the potential carving up of Iraq in a manner that would be detrimental to the interests of France's geocentric capital.

Our analysis of imperialism in the age of globalisation suggests that its defining characteristic is rent extraction by global from local. It follows that whoever or whatever is confined within a local territory (territory not defined in a geographical sense alone) will have a conflict of interest with global capital. In other words, such forces have reasons for conflict with imperialism in this age. So, perhaps the fraction of capital located within a country and from which rent is extracted using international laws and regulations may be called the national capital of this phase. An instance, which we have cited, is that of the small-scale sector. The products of this sector are confined to the domestic market, using various rules and regulations and are allowed to go global only as the property of global capital. This confinement allows extraction of rent by global capital. So, in the sense that we have defined, we can claim that small capital is part of national capital. Pharmaceutical companies owned by global capital are extracting rent from local drug companies by barring the free mobility of scientific knowledge. So, capital involved in such production may be termed national, or perhaps more appropriately, local.

Governments of many poor countries are performing as junior partners to the imperialist nations. The greater the proportionate participation of Indian capital in global capital, the greater the chances of the Indian government's performing as a full-fledged imperial nation. In recent times, our patriotic fervour has been well served by some exercise in fortune-telling, going by the acronym BRICK, which stands for Brazil Russia India China Korea. There is a prediction that these economies have the greatest growth potential in the twenty-first century. We would say that if these soothsayers were correct, then our government would emerge as a part of the senior team of imperialism in this century. As long as it remains a part of the junior team, it will advocate, however weakly, the cause of national capital. As the proportionate significance of ground rent increases, the state will find the demands of national capital to be unnecessary bother. Perhaps, at this juncture, a point that we have already made needs reiteration: even if these predictions (that is the BRICK theory) should turn out to be correct, there is no reason to expect the lot of the average Indian to improve as a consequence. Global capital, whatever be its original country label, will always be interested in keeping resources of all kinds confined within geographical territories so as to be able to extract rent.

Global Capital versus Agricultural Interests

There are various economic groups within the agricultural sector of poor nations, whose interests clash with that of global capital. The rural poor (which includes small and marginal farmers and agricultural labourers) are adversely affected in various ways by globalisation. Horticulture, orchard cultivation and the cultivation of agro-industrial inputs are taking precedence over the cultivation of foodgrains. Partly, this is explained by the lure of foreign markets. The entry of the agro-processing industry, and other reasons, all connected with globalisation, also contribute to this phenomenon. Because this leads to a fall in the supply of foodgrains in the market, the cost of living of the poor is on the rise. The cost of cultivation is increasing because of the decline in the subsidies given by the government to the producers of inputs for the agricultural sector. The small farmers are being forced into the cultivation of the more profitable commercial crops. They have little acquaintance with the market for such crops and the fluctuations in the prices of these crops depend on international price fluctuations, which these farmers have no way of predicting. So, instead of earning profit, they have to incur heavy losses in many years. The only escape from market fate is to opt out; to sell off the little cultivable land one possesses and join the exodus of the refugees of development or to commit suicide. Ownership is being concentrated. Agro-processing capital is directly entering agricultural production through a system of advances, binding farmers to produce according the dictates of dictates of this capital. To facilitate this process, the government is legalising contract farming and land ceiling laws are being relaxed to aid the process of concentration.

The changes in the agricultural sector are also adversely affecting the agricultural workers. The cultivation of crops that are being favoured by this process is less labour intensive. So, unemployment is increasing. Further, because of the rise in the prices of food crops, their cost of living is also increasing.

The current condition of the small and marginal farmers, and agricultural labourers is an unavoidable consequence of the globalisation that we have come to accept. A global market is not the playground of the local! Only when the process of dispossession/concentration has been completed will the turmoil in the agricultural sector end. Once the state has become a willing or unwilling partner in the process of globalisation, it is not in its power to intervene to even ameliorate the distress of these segments of the rural population. So the government becomes as insensitive to the fate of this rural mass, as it is about the fate of the industrial workers and urban unemployed. This is indicated by the government's anxiousness to promote the production of commercial crops, the expansion of the food-processing industry and contract farming as also by its alacrity in relaxing the ceiling on land holding size and to promote contract farming.

The creation of the Special Economic Zones (SEZ) by acquiring agricultural land has added to the woes of an already much-harassed peasantry. These SEZs are territories demarcated by the state governments with the concurrence of the central government. Enterprises located in these territories are exempted from customs duties, income, and excise taxes. The objective is to provide to global capital, within these SEZs, all the legal and economic facilities that the governments (both central and state) are committed to ultimately provide nationwide. These areas are almost entirely chosen by some global enterprise. The concerned state government then acquires the land from the farmers against payment of some meagre compensation. The peasants are resisting such virtual eviction in many places, but the state governments are threatening to use a colonial Land Acquisition Act, which allows the government to acquire any land for a 'public purpose', [6] on payment of 'compensation', even though the owner may not be willing to part with the plot. The acquired land is then handed over to the enterprise at a subsidised rate. That is, global capital has to pay just a fraction of even the meagre compensation that is given to the peasants. The creation of SEZs is, of course, part of what has been traditionally considered to constitute primitive capital accumulation.[7]

In this context it should be remembered that, in the federal set-up of India, agricultural policy is the preserve of the states, with the exception of certain areas, like inter-state trade, international trade, and fixation of minimum prices. So, in spite of repetition, we have to underscore the fact that the parliamentary left has fallen prey to the culture of the market. Though it has been in power in a state for three decades, it has not tried to think up any alternative strategy of agricultural development. The surrender of the leftists to the market is not without contradiction. While on the one hand, they are playing a leading role in initiating growth-oriented agricultural and industrial policies whose efficiency is judged by market indicators, on the other they have been adopting a number of progressive and imaginative policies relating to decentralisation of political and administrative power. One feels that the segment of the left that has not been party to this surrender has not tried to capitalise on the socio-economic possibilities created by such decentralisation. This might have taken us some distance along the path of constructing an alternative path of development and also generated public support for such a project.

We believe that the alternative can be articulated only through a practice that interweaves construction and struggle. Conflict does not mean counter-terror: terror, which opposes state terror. One has to conceive of development on the basis of existing potential. The potential for a people's development programme can only be outlined in the course of attempts at people's participatory construction, outside the realm of market hegemony. One tries to put into effect such local programmes. The existing legal framework and the attitude of the state will determine to what extent the programme can be peacefully implemented. Where the system feels threatened, conflict will be unavoidable. But the intentions of the state will then become clear to the people. Just as imposing autonomously a path of development without the informed consent of the people shows contempt for the citizens, imposing conflict on the people is also disrespectful of the aspirations of the masses. Such grand exhortations sound very good. But working out the details of an alternative development programme is a daunting task, especially since we argue for a strategy that will be based on the local conditions. There cannot be any centralised master plan for such development. It must emerge from the locality. We will discuss one such experiment, highlighting its specificities.

NOTES

1. This is part of the ongoing PhD work of Dipankar Das.
2. If an engineered variety of crop produces seeds through natural reproduction, like traditional seeds, the farmers would have to buy the seeds once only. According to the new patent laws, farmers would have to pay royalty for the use of the reproduced seeds, but this clause would be hardly enforceable for large number of far-flung farms.
3. We had discussed the postmodern critique of modernism's faith in the self-sufficiency of 'rationality', of logic. We had seen that the structure of logic itself contains appeals to rhetoric, to some kind of faith. So the faithful have to force their faith on the faithless. Market functions on the basis of clearly assigned individual property rights. Fuzzy, common property rights are not appropriate to market transactions. Neither are peasant attitudes towards land. This is a huge problem confronting the market oriented Left Front government in the state of West Bengal as it tries to convert agricultural land into industrial land. The peasant proprietor refuses to treat land as an alienable property, which can be traded in the market for commodities for money of equal worth. In this case the establishment of sole individual property right is not sufficient to commoditise land. In either case the insufficiency of logic is obvious. That is, trade is not the logical process that it is advertised as. So the state has to step in to force the logic of the marketplace. In one case it straightforward throws out the traditional, community right holders and converts land into alienable individual property. In the other case, it employs the mass organisations, subservient to the ruling parties, to persuade the peasants away from their cultural values, which preclude the sale of land. (Of course, like global capital, which uses the economic clout of the World Bank and the IMF to pressurise nations into adopting a regime of laws, regulations and economic policies suitable for the free play of global capital, but is not averse to use of brute military force if these milder weapons fail, the Left Front government is committed to forcible acquisition of land in case persuasion fails to convince the farmers to sell their lands to industrialists).
4. WTO may formally introduce labour mobility clauses, but such change will become 'binding' only in the event that global capital is certain that it has sufficient safeguards in the form of permissible visa restrictions in the name of 'terror threat, etc., in place.
5. This was a term used to designate the nature of the government

that was to assume power in states like China where the workers party led a successful revolution after the success of the socialist revolution in the Soviet Union. The capitalist class could not be relied upon to fulfil its historical task of dislodging the entrenched feudal and imperialist interests because the revolution of 1917 had made them wary of dislodging any authority through a revolution. Hence even the task of overthrowing the part feudal and part imperialist order had to be taken up by the workers party. It was not envisaged that the workers would bring about this change alone. An alliance of peasantry, national capital, and workers had to be forged under the leadership of the workers. New Democracy was the nature of the state that would come into being once this alliance had overthrown the ruling alliance of feudal elements and imperial interests. This scheme of revolutionary change was popularised by the Chinese Communist Party, particularly Mao.

6. 'Public purpose' is a vague term, which can be suitably interpreted to suit the needs of global capital. For example the government of West Bengal has used this Act to acquire land that will be handed over to the Tatas for construction of a small car factory. This has been interpreted as a private purpose because it is claimed that it will provide employment to the people of the state. Even if one does not contest the veracity of this highly improbable claim, one can still ask how the employment of workers by a profitable enterprise in order to enhance its profits can be termed as a deed with a public or social purpose.
7. We have partly discussed one particular case of such land acquisition by the state on behalf of global capital at Singur in the state of West Bengal on page 18, footnote 14. There are already at least five instances, spread over four states, where the state governments have fallen over backwards (or are well on the way) to acquire agricultural land for industrialists. Critics of this policy argue that the compensation being offered is not 'adequate', that agricultural production will go down as the proposed SEZs are largely located on prime agricultural land, that the tax exemptions offered to enterprises located in SEZs together with the loss of water cess and other payments, which the displaced farmers used to make cause heavy revenue losses to the state governments, that severe ecological damage will occur where the SEZ is located on what was originally forest land. The governments of the states are impervious to such arguments, whatever be the colour of the party in power in the state. This is

understandable. The basic thrust of all economic policy, in the age of globalisation, is towards facilitating the costless worldwide movement of global capital, while keeping labour, knowledge, technology and small production locally confined. Given this objective, no form of restriction on the saleability of land is acceptable. Thus considerations like the right to work of the displaced peasants, decline in agricultural production, revenue losses, ecological devastation are of no consequence.

SEZs are very significant features of the development path that has been chosen by India. As we have pointed out already,that the current phase of development, which has been termed 'globalisation', is based on enclave development. SEZs provide the ultimate example of enclave development. Those who can afford will live and die in the SEZs, only coming out occasionally to go to the airports to catch a flight. These will be mini cities where health, education, recreation facilities, etc., will all be available at a price. All that independent India had promised to its citizens, but failed to provide, will now be available to the glittering rich within the walls of these enclaves. Of course, the rich and famous will not have to pay the entire cost of production of the facilities that they will enjoy because the government is committed to supplying natural resources, like land and water, at no cost or at throw away prices.

8

Another Globalisation

Preliminaries

A critical analysis of globalisation is not sufficient ground for thinking of an alternative path of development (this is not to suggest that there must be a *single sufficient ground* from which a *singular* path can be imagined). For this it is necessary to explore in depth the manifold contradictions and conflicts that are internal to the system also. In this chapter we will only try to define more sharply the contours of the proposals for an alternative, which have emerged in the course of our preceding discussion. In spite of this rider, critiquing globalisation is a good ground for imagining an alternative development because, as we see it, the insoluble clashes of interests between those dispossessed by the process of globalisation and the globalised is what is causing all the headache to the barons of the global order today – the conflict between the local and the global. This is partly reflected in the worldwide escalation of conflict between inchoate groups of locals, on one side, and the globalised, on the other. This explains why gender issues, ecological concerns, and the struggle for survival of those who are literally the refugees of development are prominent on the agenda of the dissenters. These movements that are restricted to organising for limited and localised demands are a far cry from the organised leftist movements for capture of predefined state power that used to constitute the dominant protests during the period roughly between the birth of the erstwhile USSR and its demise.

The principal endeavour of imperialism in the current age is to extract rent, taking advantage of natural or imposed immobility and non-reproducibility. The reason can be found in the history of evolution of capitalism. Grossly put, since the 1970s, technology and the organisational structure of capitalist enterprise have evolved in such a way that income distribution is becoming acutely skewed. Technological innovation is directed towards reducing manpower requirement. At the same time, the need for technicians with some degree of mechanical competence in the operation of computer-aided production processes is increasing disproportionately. This technical labour force has to be compensated for the investment in acquisition of such training. Though they can hardly be differentiated from their older traditional counterpart in the labour force, in terms of their mechanical slavery to the orders of the management, they earn higher wages. For this small segment of the workforce, as well as for the expanding segment of managerial staff, salaries and wages are rising. For the large masses of the population, who cannot afford to acquire such skills, unemployment is on the rise. To maintain a demand-supply balance, sectoral division of investment is adapted to the increasingly unequal distribution of purchasing power. An increasing proportion of workforce is employed in the production of luxury goods and services. Demand has to be generated for such commodities. Esoteric needs have to be created in the minds of the small fraction of the workforce that can buy. So, there is an expansion in the workforce employed in sales and advertisement. But this is insufficient for compensating for the sluggishness of demand caused by the phenomenal decrease in the rate of growth of the demand for mass-consumption goods. The culture of the market-oriented society has mutated to the aid of sustaining/ seducing the exponentially expanding desires of the rich. An elementary aspect of this new culture is that it breeds a perception of a fast rate of obsolescence of consumer durables. This also causes a fast rate of obsolescence of technology – both of that employed in producing such commodities, as well as that embodied in the durables themselves. The cost of increasing R&D to support this fundamental systemic requirement is balanced by the accompanying reduction in labour required for production. This further adds to the trend towards decrease in the demand for mass consumer goods. Credit financing of consumer purchases is a commonly used instrument for boosting sluggish demand under the circumstances. This leads to the expansion of the financial sector dedicated to the financing consumer purchases. The small workforce employed in this segment also belongs to the developed enclave. Globalisation expands the scope of earning profit in another area – speculation. New instruments of global speculation emerge. Faced with this current phase of systemic crisis, global capital is also expanding the scope of other routes of surplus extortion, which have always been available within the system. It is increasingly falling back on the tried and tested method of investment for colonisation of resources to extract rent.

It might appear, from what we have said so far, that in the current situation the main objective of an alternative path of development should be restriction of the scope of rent extraction. In other words, ending artificially-created barriers to international mobility of labour, knowledge, science and technology should be the principal goal. But unrestricted international flows cannot be the pillars of an alternative development project. The alternative has to be explored on the ground of an alternative ethics. To clarify this position, we have to probe a little into theory and philosophy, provoke them to suggest the beginnings of an answer.

A Bit of Theory

In the ruling orthodox theory, the ideal form of market is characterised by unrestricted flow of products and inputs. This image of the market has helped to maintain the hegemony of the capitalist system within theoretical economics and various degenerate versions have had considerable influence on popular discourse. There are no communities in this mythical world. Qualitatively, all individuals have equal rights. All can own property and contract to exchange. Unlike the state in pre-capitalist societies, the state here is not biased. This state articulates and administers the impersonal laws of property and contract. Each independent individual or family owns productive resources or inputs in given quantities. Quantitative equality is not necessary for this system to work. Some own hundreds of thousands of crores of rupees of capital; some have just the ability to work. Each decision-making unit (the individual or the family) supplies these inputs in the market and the productive enterprises demand them for purchase or hire to use them for commodity production. Through the play of the forces of demand and supply, the prices of the inputs are determined in the market. This in turn determines the production technology. Where labour is in abundance and capital is scarce, there relatively wage is low. So, to achieve higher rates of profit, more labour-intensive techniques are employed. In the opposite situation, capital-intensive techniques would be chosen. The prices or rentals of inputs (determined by their demand and supply) and the pre-given distribution of inputs among the individuals define income distribution. This distribution, together with their personal preferences decides how much of each commodity each decision-making unit will demand, at various prices of that commodity. The aggregate of these individual demands gives the market demand at each price. On the other hand, the prices of inputs and the input requirements per unit of output determine the cost per unit of output. Cost of production determines the supply of output at each price of the commodity. The textbooks would have it that, as more of the commodity is produced, the cost per unit increases for various reasons. Hence, increased supply can be elicited only if a greater price is offered. The interaction of demand and supply determines equilibrium price or the price at which demand exactly matches supply. This simultaneously fixes the quantity bought and sold in the market. So, through the unbiased functioning of the market, standard problems of the economy, like what is to be produced, in what quantities, for whom, by what technology are all solved by the scientific laws of demand and supply.

It is but natural that Western philosophy or, less

pretentiously, the West's way of thinking at a particular juncture influenced greatly the conceptualisation of this individual-centric model of the economy, which is bereft of any social stratification or hierarchy. Without going deep into theoretical or philosophical discussion, one may opine that Western essentialist outlook has an innate tendency to interpret all histories (be it social history or the history of sciences) as the movement from differentiated, heterogeneous, concrete existents to a homogeneous essence which then becomes manifest in the seen or observable existents. Viewed thus, during the various phases of history, the socio-economic systems were based on hierarchically ordered, differentiated rights.[1] Gradually, through a process of historical evolution, the hierarchy of rights dissolved itself dialectically[2] (to use some jargon!) to create the modern market system based on qualitatively equal rights. The highest expression of this is the perfectly competitive market system. This is the end of history. An intellectual much revered in the West has said so in so many words.[3]

That differences and concreteness are effaced in the many manifestations of a general or universal essence is a notion born of a particular philosophy or a particular way of looking at the world. This became the dominant way of making sense ever since what has been termed as the classical age – the time when the West began reading measurable differences or order into the world around (Foucault, M., 1994). Essence is formless and so has no concrete existence. So it is expressed through particular existents. What has form is material, and so has concrete characteristics. Concreteness is the specific character of materiality. A particular application of a material object may be dependent on a particular facet or quality of that object. But all the qualities cannot be directed towards that application. The commoditiness of an object depends only on its price. Perhaps we could even say that price is the substance of its commoditiness and also its measure. Price may be high or low, but there cannot be any qualitative difference in price. It is, therefore, measurable. One cannot, on the other hand, measure the satisfaction that a poor man derives when he can feed his hungry children, who have often to go without two square meals, or the pleasure of reading a thought-provoking article. So the commoditiness of this material object can be compared with the commoditiness of that material object. But the multifaceted character of this object is not directed towards its commodity being only. So the different 'values' of the commodity cannot be indicated by its price alone. In the field of market transactions, the existent is valued by its price. But all the attributes of the existent are not dissolved in market transactions. The world is full of commodities. But it does not follow that the world is fulfilled in commodities. The corollary is an essentialist myth. This works in the service of hegemony of the capitalist market, jeopardising culture and nature, which are nothing without differences, without local specificities. Because culture, nature and such other are qualitatively different, they cannot be measured.

This conclusion can be easily anticipated intuitively. Essentialism does not admit the materiality of matter. Materiality lies in the individuality of matter. And essentialism claims that the truth of the existent or matter lies in the dissolution of its individuality or concreteness in the general or universal essence. Nature's balance is based on the local attributes of nature. Commoditisation of nature strips it of its particular attributes, metamorphosing it into just a particular form or manifestation of its marketable essence. Forests are denuded. Trees metamorphose into wood to be sold in the market to generate rent for the leaseholder.

Essentialism should be unacceptable to any materialist because it refuses to accept the materiality of matter. Essence is a delusion. What is the absolute or monist character or essence is self-sufficient. Like God. Like the Market. Like *the* Party. Whatever is self determined is, consequently, self-sufficient. Believers in the market principle hold that it is self-determining. So do the believers in God, or in *the* Party. (The italics are employed to indicate that the believers in the leftist parties think that their own party is the only true Marxist party.) But the idea of self-sufficiency is itself not sustainable on a logical plain. We have seen that commoditisation depends on primitive capital accumulation. This is based on coercion, on the abrogation of community and common rights and their replacement by individual or institutional rights. So the claim that the market is self-sufficient is a lie, deliberate or otherwise, which helps maintain the hegemonic power of the system. That is why the rentier is often disguised as a profit earner.

Ethics is born at the limit of reason. The incompleteness of reason in social relations is completed by ethical principles. Within a given framework of reasoning, an argument advanced can be right or wrong, but ethics cannot be judged. So the different structures of reason, which are supported by different ethical principles, cannot be evaluated on the basis of reason. There is a conflict or contradiction between different ethical positions, which leads to one position being opposed by another. From such conflicts and their resolution, through processes that are not reasonable, alternatives emerge. Whether the rights to water and forest resources of the *adivasis*, who had dwelt for so many generations and time immemorial on the hilly banks of the Narmada, should be respected, or the demand for big dams by the rich farmers should be given priority, cannot be decided on the basis of reason. The market(able) economists say that it can be shown on the basis of a cost-benefit analysis that the Sardar Sarovar project on the river Narmada is justified. They argue that the (capitalised) market value[4] of controlled water supply and electricity generation, which will result from the project, is greater than the (capitalised) market value of what the forest dwellers could have earned, if they were not displaced by the construction of the dam. We will not join issue over the correctness of this calculation. We will not even question by what impossible means the gains of some will be translated into compensation for the losers. The problem lies in the impossibility of the evaluation itself. Construction of big dams is part of the process of PCA. Market valuation of rights, which are trampled, to bring water and forest resources within the ambit of market transactions is impossible. The community life, nature environment, culture, which the *adivasis* have lost, is not purchased in the market. Nor does there exist any alternative against which their opportunity cost[5] can be calculated. All these are unique to the forest dwellers. So, how can one calculate their market value? At the same time, it cannot be established by reason that the right to life and livelihood of the *adivasis* is justified. Actually the two different positions are based on two sets of ethical norms. One is an alternative of the other.

A Different Ethics

One proposes, therefore, that the search for an alternative should start from this clash of ethics, from the negation of the process of PCA. We do not think that the beginnings of an alternative lie in ensuring global mobility for one who is locally confined. The entirety of what is rooted in a local space can never be globally mobile. If that were possible, then essentialism would be correct – nature, culture all have but one essence, which is expressed in market price. Culture cannot be globalised. It either dominates or is dominated. The manifestations of so-called fusion cultures involve a hierarchy between the fused cultures. I think even appreciation of a culture by one who belongs to another culture involves a relation of domination or appropriation. When we, who are urbanised, watch *chhau* dance at a *puja pandal*,[6] or when the white skin people take them abroad, it is their acrobatic skills that enthral us. We capture moments of their movements in our known frames. There is, of course, a lot of difference between the known frames of the white skin and that of Indian city dwellers. Be that as it may, the elements of symbiosis, appropriation and cultural hierarchy remain common. Globalisation of nature involves rejection of the specificity of nature, as we have argued. In other words, globalisation of those who are locally rooted amounts to uprooting them. The local community had rights over what was part of the natural balance of the locality. Actually, 'right' is a misnomer in this context. Perhaps one can say that the relation of nature with the local people was one of mutual dependence. Wood becomes the property of one who uproots the tree. This property owner appropriates rent. Trees become wood. And the one who initiates this metamorphosis after death becomes the rent-appropriating owner.

The project of constructing an alternative path of

development must stop rent extraction by the global while respecting local differences. The locally rooted working people are the bearers of these differences. Cooperative-based production must emerge from the initiative of the labouring people. And some kind of direct interaction machinery will have to be created to prevent rent extraction. The alternative globalisation that we are talking about is the globalisation of the relations between these cooperatives.

The proposal perhaps begs more questions than it answers. A basic question – why should the labouring people be the bearers of local specificity? Recall that we are not using the term 'local' in a geographical sense alone. From the point of the labouring person, specificity means the specificity of production. The production process in which one is employed indicates a working person's position. Of course, a person assumes various positions at different times. If the factory is closed down, then at least for some time, the position of a militant trade unionist becomes predominant. But the worker identity or position gradually fades. Consider one who is employed in a factory producing pesticides. The person can no longer be identified as a worker if this factory shuts down. So, if the particular region or locality, the factory, loses its specific characteristic – manufacturing pesticides – the worker ceases to exist qua worker. On the other hand, the owner of the factory is not the bearer of this local specificity. The capitalist's calculations are based on the generality of market existence, on the expression of this universal – the market price. It is with profits calculated at market prices that the capitalist is concerned. The capitalist has no qualms about shutting down a factory to construct luxury apartments on the land if this business promises greater profit. One's identity as capitalist, what we have after a fashion called capitalist class position, remains unscathed, but the working class position ceases to exist if the factory shuts down.

What if the worker gets alternative employment? If the Kanoria jute mill worker gets a job in another factory? After all, if the worker has equal facility of moving from job to job, then the mill worker's working-class position would not be jeopardised simply because a specific mill had shut down. We cannot answer this question by using the 'global (= general)/ local (= specific)' binary[7] we have been using so far. One may say that the conclusions reached on the basis of this binary need to be supplemented. They have to be supplemented by the current mutated character of global capital.

Once upon a time, Marxists used to state with great conviction that with the progress of capitalism, the need for particular skills of the workers would vanish. Technological development was directed towards this goal. The need for particular skills of the workers gradually diminishes as the skills are built into the machines. This was undoubtedly true of a certain period. But what one did not account for was capital's immense power of mutation. Capital has no fixation with any particular direction of technological progress. It has been our contention that in the age of globalisation, the principal objective of capital is to extract rent. This has determined the course along which economic laws and regulations are to be restructured, as well as the course of technological change. A principal source of rent extraction is the outsourcing of parts of business activities to areas where wages are chronically low. For this it is imperative that unemployment be maintained in the poor countries. So there is little reason to believe that if Kanoria Jute Mill shuts down, the workers will find alternative employment. The trend of technological development has adapted to the tendency of global capital being invested away from material production for mass consumption towards production of luxuries and services. Conflicts, accommodation, and supercession at various levels determine the actual path of capitalist development at every stage. Development in turn changes the nature of such conflicts and compromises. There cannot be any rule that the nature of capitalist development must be such that there will be a movement away from the employment of particular skill-dependent labour towards generalised, unskilled labour. The skills required by labour employed in the manufacture of mass-consumption goods are unsuitable in the production of luxuries and services like financial or IT services. It is unlikely therefore, that the workers employed in labour-intensive activities like jute manufacturing will find alternative employment when they are thrown out of jobs because the output combination has changed in tune with the changing pattern of income distribution and demand.

Labouring people are the bearers of the specificity of the location or sector in which they work. But their position may bring them into conflict with the specificity of some other location. Let us try to elaborate on this in the context of the location or field of natural balance. A labourer engaged in an activity that results in the destruction of natural balance cannot be the bearer of environmental balance or sustainable production. The application of chemical pesticides harms environmental balance. So the labourer employed in the production of pesticides cannot be the bearer of natural balance of the environment.

There are various other sites of conflict that one can imagine, just a priori, in the process of articulation of the local working people's community/cooperative initiative. When this question was being discussed at a recent seminar on people's movements,[8] it was pointed out that experiments with direct democracies at the village level had failed because of the conflicts between even the different fractions of the working people within a village.[9] In such circumstances, established political parties – left and right; parliamentary and extra-parliamentary – step in to pervert such experiments.

The characteristic of a factory is to be productive. The bearer of this characteristic is the labourer engaged in the factory. The characteristic of agricultural land is to produce agricultural crops. That is why, when the government takes over agricultural land for construction of industry or amusement parks, the peasants oppose such moves. Does it mean that upholding the local in the face of global implies one is opposed to all change, to the production of new goods and services, to all relocation of labour? No. But we do insist on the need for working out a participatory change. Even the development of science and technology is responsive to the power structure. So a cooperative relation must grow between science and technology and an alternative development. It is now almost a cliché that education and the pursuit of knowledge and science must be adapted to the needs of production. I would not disagree. But, I would say that the slogan needs to be made more specific: the relation must be cooperative. In the present situation, this slogan simply amounts to the demand that education, knowledge and science must all be subservient to the needs of global capital. A lot of educationists seem quite happy to accept a functional role for education. What we are proposing, on the other hand, is that there should not be a hierarchy in the relation between education and material production.

An Economist's Defence

A plausible defence of our plea for an alternative development based on the 'local community' can partly be based in economics, without referring to the limit of logic itself.[10] Let us argue this through a parable.[11]

In the primitive West there were the Adams and the Eves. They were politically as incorrect as the West has forever been. The Adams hunted and the Eves cooked. The hunters' tools and the cooks' hearth were both primitive. So they produced just enough to live. That is, they did not produce any surplus. On an average, each Adam hunted two deer and each Eve cooked two deer. For simplicity, we assume that there were equal number of Adams and Eves. The needs of the hunters and the cooks were recognised as different. It was deemed that the activity of hunting required greater expenditure of energy than the activity of cooking. Hence greater replacement of muscle and sinew was necessary. So the hunters were each to be provided with 1½ cooked deer, while each cook was to be provided with ½ cooked deer. There was peace and equilibrium.

Adams improved their tools and Eves their hearth. Now, four deer were hunted on an average by each Adam and four deer were cooked by the average Eve. So now there was a surplus of two cooked deer for each pair of Adam and Eve. The question is: what to do with this surplus? Could it be distributed by the same rule as that for distribution of subsistence? In other words, could Adam be allotted three cooked deer and Eve one? This would close the issue and generate the economist's equilibrium. But why should Eve accept a smaller share of the surplus? Eve accepted a smaller share of subsistence because her need was smaller. But there is no reason for her to willingly accept a smaller share of the surplus. Couldn't the surplus be distributed equally? Possibly. But that would be a different rule. The point we are getting at is that production of surplus calls for the generation of a different rule for its appropriation and distribution than the rule for distribution of subsistence. In all historical societies, this rule has been imposed by a group of functionaries separate from those who produce the surplus. The latter are termed the surplus-producing or exploited class by Marx. The former group, which functions both as the administrator of the rule and also the appropriator of surplus, is termed the exploiting class. It is conceivable that the two functions may be merged in a part of the surplus-producing class. This would happen, for example, if the Adams could impose the rule of dividing the surplus two cooked deer in the same proportion in which the subsistence was distributed so that each Adam got 1½ of the surplus and each Eve got ½.

Marxists used to dream of a day when there would no longer be class distinctions. Given the inevitability of the functional separation, this dream can be realised only on the condition that both functionaries are bound together ethically and morally in the same community. There has to be a consensus regarding the productive utilisation of the surplus. A consensus has to be based on a communion – on a community.

It is precisely the absence or the failure of the effort to construct this community that explains the failure of socialist construction. Because of the difficulty of the project, the effort to construct the physical being of the community has been displaced by the easier project of the mediated community. The party has become the physical mediator between the surplus producers and the idea of the community. The party has manifested itself in the form of the party and government/ enterprise bureaucrats. They have/had taken over the function of directing the production and utilisation of the surplus in the name of the community of working people. At the core of the failure of socialist construction lies the failure to construct a community of working people that performs these two functions. This has been technically referred to as the problem of ignoring democracy in the working of the principle of democratic centralism. While the function of devising and administering the rule for production and utilisation of surplus has been centralised, the function of producing surplus has been spread out among the locals. Attempts to 'reform' the system have uniformly consisted of interpreting 'democracy' as giving greater autonomy of deciding the production and utilisation of surplus to the enterprise level functionaries who decide these issues. As a corollary, the planning apparatus has been replaced with market signals. This has no implication for the loss of the Marxist dream. Deification of efficiency in terms of market prices that has accompanied such reforms have certain implications that can de elaborated in terms of the two faces of capitalism that we have explained in the context of the difference between the roles of the IMF and WTO on one hand, and the World Bank on the other. While the planned system was more like the benevolent face of capital, the post-reform system is more consistent with the White, Christian, Male face of capital.

Neither could perform the fundamental task of eliminating the distance between the two sets of functionaries. The two functions can be accommodated within a non-exploitative system in the sense that Marxists were supposed to dream about only on condition that a community is constructed that discharges both the functions of surplus production and of planning its production and utilisation. This community has to be constructed even as functionaries come together in the course of production. It has to be a simultaneous process – a process of construction and struggle.

Let us go back to our parable. There was a problem with the distribution of the surplus two cooked deer that were produced per pair of Adam and Eve in the community. We talked of that. But there is a problem even before that with our narrative that we silently skipped. The community was doing OK, producing according to their subsistence requirements. Why go for producing more and open the floodgates to so many problems? The only logical way I can see the narrative develop is to assume that the community talked and quarrelled and finally concluded that they *needed* to produce the surplus. But then, don't needs relate to subsistence and isn't surplus a totally different kettle of fish according to what we have argued? When we equated needs with subsistence, we were arguing within cultural idioms of hedonistic individuals – the kind that is vividly presented in neoclassical textbooks as neither inheriting nor bequeathing. But when we talk in the idioms of community, needs do not relate to the individuals who make up the community now and further, it does not relate to the present only. The community thinks of its own future as also of the future of its children. Quite simply, in our stylised example, the community might decide to produce more to keep something by for the winter months. Or it may decide to keep something by for the mouths that are in the wombs of the Eves.

All this really boils down to the need for constructing local communities that will bridge the gap between the two unavoidably different economic functions that have to be performed in a surplus-producing economy. Using jargon that is currently in favour, one can say that there are inevitably two positions that exist within the economic space once surplus is produced. These positions are inherently contradictory if separated and divided between two different groups of functionaries that are not related in any way save because of the complementarity of the roles of surplus production and its management and appropriation. The community that binds the two groups of functionaries has to be 'local' not 'global' because the global community is an idea that cannot physically exist in the sense of the members actually empathising with the other concrete members. We are not pleading for isolationalism, though that is a positive pitfall to guard against. The broader community can meaningfully be born out of the constructive interaction of these local communities. Without the practice of such construction through struggle, the very notion of the communion between the surplus-producing position and the position of those who plan the production and utilisation of the surplus would not coalesce. That is, the ethics of this community cannot be worked out and so imbibed in the morality of the members.

Some Problems

This proposal for exploring alternatives is in a rather inchoate state and, therefore, likely to be confused with various kinds of civil society movements. A possibility that is rather unpalatable is to be equated with radical environmentalists. So let us mark at least some of our distance from them. They have a tendency to forget history and present some position in time as if it was the original, unsullied, natural situation. So, when one talks of 'locality', one must remember that it is also the result of some complex historical process through which some communities had been displaced. At a meeting convened to protest against the environmental degradation of Santiniketan and its surrounding areas, Medha Patkar reminded the agitators of the history of Santiniketan. She was one with the resistance to the current attempts to destroy the ecological balance or the human-nature balance of the region. But she pleaded that the agitators should be sensitive to the fact that their claims to the status of 'original inhabitants' was established by abrogating the rights of the *adivasis* who previously dwelt in parts of this settlement. The current natural and demographic structure has a history, which includes displacement of *adivasis* and spoilation of a past natural balance. The attempt to disown history or the complex process that has brought the present into being may work in favour of some self-seeking interests.

Just as we should not disown history, so also we cannot reject the present. Modern development creates refugees of development by constructing industry or housing resorts for the rich on agricultural land; by the irreplenishable loss of fertility caused by modern farming; by the loss of occupation of the fishermen caused by the discharge of chemical effluents into water bodies; by the displacement of forest dwellers and agriculturists on account of construction of large dams. The displaced crowd cities in search of livelihood. They construct marginal communities in the 'illegal' shanties lining railroads, leaving behind old settlements, old community identities. They find odd jobs in the unorganised sector, remain unemployed or engage themselves in 'anti-social' activities to eke out a living.

They form new communities. Their desires and demands change. We cannot turn back the wheels of this inhuman progress by rejecting the present. To which past shall we return? Which historical situation shall we designate as original? We have to start from the present, from the current demands of the labouring communities. This must be the starting point of the movement to construct a cooperative human psyche, so that one day the worker in the armaments factory will also march for peace. The alternative does not lie in the imposition of some leadership's dreams and schemes, ignoring the present demands of the community of working people, which are expressed mainly in their economic struggles. Rather, one can attempt to delimit the scope of market centrism by joining in the economic struggles of such communities. If one can mobilise public pressure to compel the government to increase its social welfare spending, for example, the orientation of health and education towards the demands of market-worthy individuals may be partly balanced.

The little that we have been able to articulate by way of an alternative to the devastating course of globalisation just constitutes a preliminary proposal based on a theoretical understanding. It has no pretension to constituting a plan of action, however sketchy. Indeed, such cannot be the product of an intellectual exercise, individual or collective. There is reason for this inability that ties up with the outlines of our vision, which we have sketched. We are not proposing *local* as simply the negation of *global*. The community on which the alternative course of human development has to be based is not wholly defined as what is not global. It has to have a positive content that can manifest itself through the process of conscious construction of the local on the basis of the aspirations of the local working people. We will discuss in some detail in the next chapter one such experiment that was begun at Chhattisgarh and continues to be a source of inspiration to us.

Let us end this chapter on a self-critical note. The proposal is for the construction of a different economy and society based on an alternative set of ethics. Ethics is born of morality (though in turn the former constitutes the latter), which is constituted in the process of living, of dreaming, of dreaming of a different living. But we have based our proposals on our theoretical analysis. Analysis is inevitably limited by the categories it uses, by its structure of logic. Categories spring traps which analysis cannot avoid. But an alternative ethics can be established only by transcending the categories of the dominant culture, which cloud our thoughts. Transcendence occurs through the daily conflicts of our life. Transcendence is a process, which the dominant categories cannot capture, analysis cannot pin down. It occurs in our desires, which build, and are built, into our dreams. If it were an analytical process, then intellectuals could competently draw up blueprints of social change. Certain terms that we have deployed in this paragraph indicate our inability to theorise transcendence in the same way as we theorise materiality. Terms like 'cloud', dreams', 'desires', 'cooperative relation', etc. are terms that we do not use as economists.

Our proposal for an alternative rests largely on a binary – general/specific. Unfortunately, in spite of trying to evade the issue through various linguistic juggleries, one is forced to admit, at the end of the day, that ultimately, a major lacuna of all analytical explorations of the nature of society is the inability to transcend binary thought categories. The particular binary that we have deployed has its own limitations. We have said that the labouring people are the bearers of their local specificity. We have advanced some arguments in support of this proposal. But even an exploitative class with a localised power base is a bearer of local specificity in some sense. The landed aristocrats, say the zamindars, extracted /extract feudal rent on the basis of feudal landed property rights over a defined territory. So this lord was/is the bearer of local values. It follows that we are not proposing an alternative based on the dreams and desires of the labouring people simply because they are the agency of the local. *Faith in the working people is an autonomous, fundamental characteristic of our position.* This, as we have argued in the immediately preceding section, follows from the dream we share with Marx.

Proposing the concrete, which has a specific character that cannot be dissolved in any generality or essence, against a faceless entity that dissolves into a particular manifestation of an essence, may lure the analysis into some snares. We often tend to ignore the existence of a power structure at the level of the local community. Though our faith in the working people is an autonomous position, there is a sense in which the local working people are bound to be more committed in their struggle against the dehumanising development that is called globalisation than the surplus appropriator whose power is based on the locality. The powerful have greater adaptability to the changing social and economic environment that is inclining increasingly towards globalisation. In that sense, they are always less steadfast in their opposition to globalisation than the local working people. An instance from the recent history of India would sustain our position. The dispossession of farming communities to acquire land for industry has drawn a lot of flack from various quarters for different reasons. The organised resistance of the peasants – mainly the small landholders, the sharecroppers, and the landless labourers – stalled the fond projects of the various state governments for industrialisation at the cost of agriculture. Among the different groups of local protestors, the landless labourers and the sharecroppers were the most resilient. The larger landowners were the ones who were among the first to give up their claims to land against the promise of compensation. They were, presumably, the best able to make sense and profit outside their local, rural world. Our hope is that the local working people's cooperatives will be able to transcend local sectarianism also. One must, of course, be constantly alive to the other possibility.

We should be watchful about the limitations of using the 'general/concrete' binary or the related 'global/local' binary. It may lead to positions that are based on some sort of 'archeo-teleological pathos', like the position of the radical environmentalists. But we should also be conscious that in the age of globalisation, the greater danger lies in being blinded by the seduction of the global, which includes, among other devices, the glorification of universality against the tyranny of the locality. Globalised production and consumption are not conditioned by any societal norms. This is the obverse side of consumerist culture. When the value of output is reduced to a generalised value – value in the market – there is no scope for society to exercise any kind of moral control. As far as the value to society is concerned, there is no distinction between 200kg of paddy and a 'designer' shirt, as long as they both sell at Rs.2000 in the market. Both would contribute the same to the Gross National Product of the country. The concept of economic demand becomes important in this context. 'Demand' in a market economy refers to need or desire backed with the power to fulfill it through purchase in the market. The market has no means of registering 'need'; it can only record 'demand'. If a poor family does not have the money to buy the 200kg of rice – with which it could have staved off starvation for, say, six months – whereas a rich man has the power to satisfy his fashion fancy and buy the shirt, the market is quite unconcerned. The market would not know that the poor family has a desire to live! In fact, as we have mentioned, the harsh individualistic culture (which we have called White, Christian, Male) that sustains support for the market, would find this refusal to judge the need to survive as intrinsically superior to the desire to satisfy a whim to be ethically correct. If the survival of the poor family had been desired by the society, the family would have earned sufficient income by selling the resources at its command in the market. So, if you have the money, whatever you buy is justified according to market norms. This attitude breeds unfettered consumerism.

Building the alternative will entail, among other things, recovering humanism, a concern for others in society, which has been buried deep under decades of market hedonism. The alternative does not consist of just changing the policies of the government. We will all have to participate in the construction of a new humanity and a society. It is but inevitable that global capital and the state will resist the construction of the alternative – cooperative construction, that is. Counter—resistance in self-defence will follow. The details of the alternative will ultimately be worked out in the course of this construction and struggle. *Nirman aur sangharsh*, which is also *sangharsh aur nirman*.

NOTES

1. For example, in the Grecian city civilisations there were the citizens, who had the freedom to decide their occupation as well as the right to vote. Then there were the freemen who had the right to decide their occupation but did not have the right to vote. And there were the slaves who, as property of their owners, had no right.
2. That is, through a process which has certain similarities with the process of dialogue. One puts forward a position. Another criticises this position, pointing out what has been left out of consideration. One then modifies, or improves the original position to accommodate the counter position. The first position is what is called the 'thesis'; the counter position is the anti-thesis. And the final position is the synthesis. The rationalist sees the course of history as also a similar process. The so-called 'spirit of history' evolves in this dialectical manner, and we, the actors, are the passive agents of this spirit. This is also, more or less, the position taken by the orthodox Left. We will later discuss this particular process of dialectics in some greater detail.
3. Fukuyama, Francis, 1992.
4. Capitalised value means the current market value of anticipated future earnings, or the amount of current rupees, which is as valuable as the stream of expected future earnings. This calculation is based on the rate of interest. To clarify, let us take the help of a grossly simplified example. If the rate of interest were 10%, then Rs.100 lent out today would amount to Rs.110, a year hence. We would say that the capitalised value of Rs.110 of the next year is Rs.100.
5. Opportunity cost is the cost of opportunities sacrificed in choosing one situation. For example, a person chooses to renounce a fat salaried job to go to the forest to live the life of a hermit. The monetary value of this latter life cannot be directly calculated, because the means of this life are not purchased in the market. But one can say that, it must be at least as valuable to this person as the fat salary that was sacrificed. This salary would be the opportunity cost of the life of the hermit.
6. Temporary, highly decorative structures built to house the Hindu deities during the period of their worship (and accompanying revelry) as assigned by the religious almanac. These are mostly community festivals, which serve a secular purpose of bonding the community. In the urban areas, populated by Hindus – professing or nonprofessing – these are almost the sole events in

which the locality participates as a body. There are regional variations in the order of popularity of the deities. For example, *Ganesha* is the favourite in Western India, *Durga* in eastern India, etc.. The locality organises cultural programmes and community meals during the ritual period, which is often extended to suit the degree of merriment generated.

7. Discourse or discussions of ways of thinking, or ways of conceptualising, recognise certain general principles which are widely used to make sense to oneself and also to others (when communicating). One such principle is the binary principle. For example, 'inanimate' makes sense only in contrast to 'living'. These two terms constitute a binary.
8. Organised by the Indian Academy of Social Sciences at Kolkata on Nov. 3, 2007.
9. The specific example was the *Gram Committees* formed to resist land acquisition at Nandigram, a region in the district of Medinipur in West Bengal, for construction of industries. These committees had been organised on the principle of direct democracy by the inhabitants of the region, with the active participation of local grass root activists of various parties, immediately after word got around that land had been earmarked for construction of a 'chemical hub' in that region. These committees had resorted to violent resistance to entry of police and government. Soon afterwards, the leading opposition in the state legislature together with some extreme left elements had, in the name of giving organisational shape to the movement, formed the Bhumi Ucched Pratirodh Committee with representatives of various political parties. This was not surprising. What was surprising was that the Gram Committees were very soon rendered non-functional and superseded by the BUPC. It was suggested by many at the workshop that political parties easily exploit the internal conflicts of an existing community to subvert experiments with community based action – whether it be of resistance or of construction. Their interest is clear. Success of such initiative would challenge their position as mediators of democracy.
10. This question of logic and its limit is not posed rigorously here. We have throughout attempted to present issues of theory and philosophy in a way that does not daunt the uninitiated reader. This is a question of philosophy that is raised here. In fact we say can argue for construction of local community in counter position to global capital within the domain of economic logic, because

the way we open up this domain really questions its logical self sufficiency. Its self-adequacy, so to say. What we are proposing is what has been proposed in the overdetermined Marxist theory. It is that there is no self-sufficiency of any particular field of social interaction. As we shall argue, ever since surplus has been produced there have been two contradictory positions within the economic field. The closure or the temporary balance between these can be affected only through a political solution. There is another interesting way in which the question of super adequation of the economic theoretical space has been raised. It is in terms of the super adequation of labour power within the Marxist analysis: labour power commodity producing more value than its own value. This is the reason for its ability to source value within the Marxist scheme. (Spivak, 1985)

11. The idea of this parable is contained in Chaudhury(2001). It was further elaborated in Basu (2001)

9

Tracing the Roots

A Dream Dissipated

A critique of the destructive path of 'development', that is globalisation, needs to be rooted in a vision of the alternative. The entrenched left has failed to evolve any alternative. In fact, it has long abandoned the search. It has forgotten to dream. Its policies are quite unabashedly based on pragmatism. Partly, the defeat, in one case, and the confusing state, in the other, of what used to be looked up to as the international centres of socialism accounts for the unimaginative surrender of the established left to global capital's hegemony.[1] Partly, it is because of their inability to come to terms with, that is to negotiate with, bourgeois liberty or democracy, generally, and more particularly with parliamentary power, that most of these parties have become preoccupied with 'performance' defined by the system. Politically, such performance is defined by success at the hustings. Where they run the governments it is defined economically by the success of states, as measured by market indicators. Achievement in terms of these indicators has become the obsession of these parties. The party leadership deifies this as pragmatism, as opposed to left adventurism. Perhaps, the dreams and visions have been displaced into these goals through some psychological process, which is beyond my competence to attempt understanding. Perhaps, it is a question of substitute gratification. This really implies that the entrenched left also frames its plans and programmes under the hegemony of capital. Whatever be the process of this transmogrification, the passionate desire of the rank and file of these parties to achieve these ends has made the party organisations into automatons ruthlessly pursuing these objectives, without knowing, or caring to know, how these relate to whatever is leftism. The core having been rendered hollow, unflinching, unquestioning commitment to these substitute passions, and blind discipline, have become the indices of politicisation of the cadre. This has made the party apparatus a huge monolith swallowing up all spaces where dissent, or at least criticism, could emerge. It has also rendered this apparatus into a frightening spectre of brutal intolerance wherever it has been able to retain power for a substantial length of time.

Complementing this leftism is the leftism at the other extreme. To this strand of leftism also, state power is the sole object of struggle. But, while the left in power organises to win/retain power through the existing electoral process, the ultra left tries to capture power solely through armed conflict. There is no realisation within this variety of left that the struggle for state power and the struggle for its transformation should not be two separate movements, but part of the same symbiotic process. To them, state power is a defined and visible object waiting to be captured. These groups are organised along military lines, they are trained to abjure criticality. Discipline and so, a lack of criticality, have become their guiding organisational principle also. This renders these organisations no less mechanical, intolerant and fundamentalist than the parliamentary left. This strand of the left is as much under the sway of global capital's cultural hegemony as the left in power. The strict separation of state from civil society[2] is a myth of the capitalist order. The imagination of the 'extreme left' of which we are talking is clouded by this myth in as much as they take state power to be given – waiting for them to capture it while the ethos and morality of the people can be left aside or taken care of through some variant of thought police.

What we are arguing for, on the other hand, is a practice, which simultaneously evokes a vision of the future, and fleshes it out in the course of practice here and now. We are proposing that a space to dream of a society founded on the working people's aspiration for equality can be reinvented, only on condition that we break the shackles of order and logic, with which the mythology of the market has so firmly tied up our minds. This myth has successfully erased the space of imagination.[3] In this age of globalisation, the global is the committed bearer of the myth. It is inscribed in its very body and bodily accessories as it flows in and out of the local spaces, with the ebb and flow of 'free trade', seducing the local, sometimes threatening it with its divine difference, assigning it to the *subcity* from which it does not forget to reap the surplus.

In the discussion in the previous chapters, we have argued that the self-sufficiency of the capitalist market as the coordinator of free decisions of qualitatively equal individuals is a myth. We have seen that there are yawning gaps in the 'logic' of the market that can only be sutured with force. Broadly, in the era of globalisation the overriding character of this force is that it is the power of the global to extract rent from the local. So we propose locality as the space in which the working class dream can be reinvented; and the locally circumscribed working people as the bearers of this dream. But locality and self-consciousness, which together determine the 'ought' of the identity of the working class, have to be simultaneously, and in an articulated manner, evoked through constructive practice.

It is in this context that the concept of capitalist rent becomes important. It is not some outlandish semantic jugglery we have been indulging in, as is the wont with us academics. The concept highlights the irrationality at the base of capitalism, giving the lie to the myth of fair play and scientific character of the market. Through its articulation with the concept of primitive capital accumulation, it shows that imperialist occupation of local territories is necessary for the sustenance of global capital. Simultaneously, it points to the limitations of individualism, to the impossibility of any ahistorical notion of the individual. It helps us to focus on the ideological use of the notions of individualism and individual liberties for maintaining the hegemony of global capital. In opposition, therefore, it also underlines the need for invoking the local community, of defining it anew, in the struggle against globalisation as imperialism of this age. It gains additional significance from its ability to show up the limitation of what is nostalgically still referred to as national capital.

Reviving a Dream

Construction and struggle – this is a tradition, which has been articulated within the practice of the Indian left also, call it Marxist if you will. This was the vision of the political movement in the Chhattisgarh region under the inspirational leadership of Shankar Guha Neogi in the 1970s and 1980s. In quite a straightforward way, the project is also related to Mao and Gramsci's imaginative interventions on Marxist theory and practice. In spite of fundamental differences, there is also a definite kinship with the ideas propagated by some nationalists like Tagore and Gandhi. Perhaps not surprisingly, given the context of the international movements that rocked the world just before the 1980s, the liberation project inaugurated at Chhattisgarh has affinity with the project of the so-called 'situationalists'[4] who were in the forefront of the movement that rocked Paris in 1968-69. This obviously relates our proposal to the postmodern geographers, especially Edward Soja and Lefebvre. It is not a matter of asserting our pedigree, which impels us to acknowledge these traditions. It is because names are short hand for a lot of ideas and dreams of whose relevance to the current context we may be just dimly aware.

'Construction' signifies the need for positively defining the local. Local is not just the negative of global. The construction that was visualised was not just of society but also of self. And not of one or the other, but as a symbiotic process. We are aware that we are not talking of predetermined class positions, of capture of given state power, but of defining self-class-community in and through an interwoven process of becoming. To provoke: construction is a process and a definition in process always implies boundaries in flux. So, 'construction and struggle' also calls for (and this is a big claim) rethinking the categorical itself, rethinking boundaries and bondage itself. We have to confront the question: 'whether positing the autonomy of the economic, the political, or even the cultural is not a part of the hegemonic project of global capital?' As a result, the question of state power and its capture have to be displaced to a terrain, which is unfamiliar to the practice of Marxism or, more precisely, to the practice of the leftist parties. It is an ethico-political question.

To paraphrase Neogi, it is in the process of cooperative production based on local conditions that the working people within a locality become conscious of their own potential. This emphasis on consciousness as an autonomous moment in the ethical life of the working class, which is also constitutive of the class itself, is an influential reading of Gramsci (Bobbio, R., 1979), though this is not an uncontested reading. Neogi was obviously inspired by Mao, particularly on the point of insisting on the physical leadership of the working people at every stage of the movement and on the point of continuous, critical evaluation of self-consciousness by the 'leadership'.[5] There are also points of similarity with certain strands of what has been dubbed as 'rural communitarian' thought[6] in the late nineteenth and early twentieth-century India. This is particularly true of those who have been perhaps less concerned with a pre-given nation's freedom than with constructing the free community. We will talk of Tagore and Gandhi in this context.

Shankar Guha Neogi

Let us read Neogi in the context of 'Problems of Trade Union Movement', '...a system based on class exploitation can only be eliminated through a struggle to establish an alternative social system *anchored in an emerging organisation of production based on the human resources of the region*, tailored to the needs of the local population, through the proper utilisation of local resources. Trade unions have not even thought of any *creative venture* in this direction' (Basu P. and Sanyal, S.,1992, p.58). Further on, he says, 'Not the bleak economism which shows no promise of a future, together with and in our economic struggles we wish to see the light of liberation, the emergence of a self-respecting working class, the fresh air of a new and distilled culture; we want a revolutionary trade union' (ibid, p. 58; translation by authors, italics added).

Neogi's own writings are few and far between. To understand the novelty of the Chhattisgarh experience, we have to rely on commentaries written largely by outsiders who were involved in the movement. Purnendu Basu has detailed the evolution of Neogi's ideas and simultaneously that of the various interrelated movements in the Chhattisgarh belt in the commemorative piece – 'One who has touched the sky with his feet on the ground' (ibid, p. 217).

In the formative phase of the movement itself, the significance of the question of local versus global was internalised in the movement. Neogi was alive to the fact that the roots of Marxism were embedded in foreign soil. There was need to indigenise its practice. To arouse the people of Chhattisgarh, their identity had to be revitalised. Towards this end it was essential to first organise the steel and mine workers, as they were the most modernised section of the local working population. So the *Chattisgarh Mine Sramik Sangh (CMSS)* was formed. Clearly, though Neogi was a great admirer of Gandhi, his idea of resurrecting the local was significantly different from that of Gandhi. In sharp contrast to Gandhi (and Tagore), Neogi's emphasis was on the working class, on arousing its aspirations. His initial thrust was towards organising the mine workers, rather than the steel workers because the latter being mainly comprised of immigrants, were unlikely to empathise with a movement which focused on the need to oppose the local to the global. Two factors that differentiated this mine worker's union from other trade union organisations need to be stressed: *right from inception workers were physically in the leadership; and the union was organised on the novel principle that it was concerned with all 24 hours of a worker's day not just with the 8 hours that the worker spent in the factory.* Workingclass consciousness was not to be limited to the attitude of the worker towards the capitalist alone. In other words, the union was concerned with lifetime as well as with labour time. This resulted from the apprehension that the enhanced purchasing power of the workers was likely to be absorbed in pandering to the growing consumerism of the workers. The movement for prohibition in the region was motivated by this concern. The women spearheaded this movement. This aspect of the movement brought to the fore three distinguishing features of this trade union. First, it emphasised a founding principle of this movement, namely that the union had to be concerned with both the lifetime as well as labour time. Second, it highlighted the awareness that the worker should not be defined on the basis of the culture of individualism – the worker was defined in the over-determined totality within which the family was a principal site or field of relations. From this concern followed the third characteristic. It was realised by the union that the nature of the involvement of women in the family made it easier for them, compared to the male members, to grasp certain aspects of the conditions of existence that were imposed on the working class. In these concerns one can see an attempt to define a working-class consciousness in the course of the movement. The movement realised that the working class could not be defined sans community. And the community and class were both constructed in the course of cooperative social construction in a particular geographical territory. So was born Chhattisgarh Mukti Morcha (CMM).

Under the aegis of the Morcha, constructive movements in the fields of education, health and environment were launched. The basic idea, which motivated these efforts, was that the alternative or people's development had to be based on the locality and created, as far as practicable, through people's efforts. The movement was conscious that all people's struggles should look forward to a constructive project. This would rid the unions of populist opportunism, like condoning job shirking and at the same time sketch pieces of the big picture of the alternative process of development, which should be the ultimate goal of left movements.

Punyabrata Goon has documented the 'People's Health Movement in Dalli-Rajhara' (ibid. p. 172). Why did a trade union take on itself the task of building a '*Shahid Haspatal*' (martyr's hospital)? The reason can be traced to its basic philosophy of 'construction and struggle'. On the one hand, struggle to change the social order, and on the other and together with it, undertake small experimental projects for cooperative construction. These could involve material construction (which leads to construction of consciousness) like the construction of a health centre or a school, or could involve construction of consciousness/ awareness (which leads to improvement in material well-being) like the campaign for preservation of the environment or the campaign for boycotting liquor. The history of the people's health movement and the subsequent construction of the *Shahid Haspatal* reflect in quite some detail the practice of this way of looking at political economy. The health movement was part of the campaign to build consciousness or, if you will, to teach the working people to dream of the future. The sincerity of involvement can be gauged from the fact that there was, initially, a heated controversy regarding the need for constructing a hospital. Those opposed to the scheme argued that this step would imply a regression to reliance on curative medicine rather than on preventive medicine. And curative medicine was touted by global capital, even consciously crippling indigenous knowledge about a preventive environment. We will not detail the debate, mentioning it only to highlight the success that the movement enjoyed at least for a limited period of time in terms of exciting the people to dream, to will the future. But one point needs to be stressed. The primary concern of this aspect of the movement was with generating awareness, with prevention, not with building infrastructure, even with cooperative effort. The idea was to reclaim for the local a territory that it had not only lost, but which had systematically been obliterated from folk memory (that of traditional preventive medicine) in order to widen the territory of capital, for its rent-seeking activity. This is the kind people's initiative against global capital's rentier exploitation that we have been talking about. Ultimately, a double-storeyed hospital, with 40 beds and a modern operation theatre and all the necessary accessories, was built entirely with the contributions – both monetary and in terms of voluntary labour – of the local working people. Even an ambulance was acquired. The process of construction and its subsequent administration is instructive. The control of both processes remained firmly in the hands of the workers, though doctors and trained nurses who worked here were outsiders who were motivated by the politics of the movement. The workers were all encouraged to participate in both the mental and physical labour involved in building and running the hospital.

The people's movement for education was also motivated by the same concerns. Not even a single child from the family of a worker had passed Class Ten when the movement started. In the course of the movement, they became aware of the effectiveness of education, both for improving their individual economic condition as well as for the movement. Twenty school buildings were established with voluntary financial and labour contributions of the workers. Most of these were handed over to the government as educational infrastructure, but the union itself ran a few.

One can think of supplementing the experience of the Chattisgarh Mine Sramik Sangathana (CMSS) with the experience of organisations like the Kerala Sastha Shahitya Parishad (KSSP) in Kerala and Ekalabya in Bhopal (to mention just a few) to envision a people's education movement which, like the people's health movement, can think of reclaiming another space that has been appropriated by global capital for rent extraction. In fact, education is turning out to be one of the most fertile areas for rent extraction in this century.

The movement for construction/appropriation of autonomous spaces out of the field from which rent is extracted by global capital must not be turned into a fetish. While these experiences establish the possibility and worth of cooperative construction by the workers here and now, the space of conventional trade union activity must not be abdicated; rather, it must be enriched by the vision that emerges from the constructive action of the working people. To cite an example, contrary to the wisdom being currently disseminated by some intellectual leftists, through a more than willing media, there is no acceptable reason for trade unions to renege on their current opposition to the efforts of the government to privatise public sector organisations. The standard argument of market-enabled leftists is that such trade union populism breeds a tribe of privileged workers who enjoy great economic advantages over the rest of the workers. It is also sometimes argued that this constitutes basically a rent-earning activity, which deprives the worker, particularly in the unorganised sector, of jobs. It is true that the extra earning of the worker in this sector constitutes rent earning of these workers. But this is not a sufficient ground for opposing the claims of the trade unions. We have argued that rent signals the limit and therefore the limitation of capital's logic. It is the ground on which the power play of global capital is obvious. But there is no reason to oppose the flow of rent away from global capital towards any segment of the working people, which is possible if the existing hierarchy of this power play can be reversed. For example, if an indigenous people somehow succeed in establishing their 'sui generis' claims on local traditional knowledge and on local, natural resources, and extracts rent for allowing access of global capital to such inputs, one should hail it as a victory of the local over the global. Ideally, we would oppose rent and exclusive rights over knowledge. But within the space of the globalised economy (even if it can be restricted by the efforts of the local working people), based on the commoditisation of all resources, the best that can be hoped for the labouring people in the immediate future, is perhaps, that they can manoeuvre to gain or retain access to some resources. Typically, the trade union extracts rent by limiting access to jobs. If the power of the trade unions was curbed, the 'logic' of the market would take over, and in a labour-surplus economy like ours, wage would plummet to less than 'living' wages. This should be the logical extension of this argument of these 'pragmatic leftists'. While this position may be perfectly acceptable to some leftists, particularly of the governmental variety, who now argue quite glibly that this or that is unavoidable because the market so commands, in our scheme this is not defensible because, to us, the market system itself is not logical. That it is a self-sufficient 'rationally' ordered system is a myth. Besides, as Neogi argued in the context of the disagreement between those in favour of building a hospital and those who thought that this would conflict with the emphasis of the people's health movement on preventive therapy, a movement cannot start from a position, which is not felt by those participating in the movement. If at this stage of the trade union movement, workers are inclined towards economic demands only, then the movement must start from those demands and build the dream of the future from these beginnings. Else, there is every possibility of the movement going the way of most left movements, where the cadre become disciplined soldiers carrying out the orders of the 'visionary' leadership.

Rural Communitarians: Gandhi and Tagore

One can try to guess the intellectual-political sources, which inspired Shankar Guha Neogi, and simultaneously read one's own prejudices into Neogi!

Gandhi was clearly an important light. So was Tagore. There are serious differences between Neogi's teaching and that of Gandhi, some of which we will elaborate on as we go along, but the ideas of 'rural communitarianism', cooperative production, and the need for building self-reliance, have obvious parallels in Gandhi. Even though Gandhi was the prophet of non-violence, he did not shy away from the potential of conflict between the state of independent India and those pursuing the communitarian projects, as has been mentioned by Chatterjee (Chatterjee, P., 1986). Apart from the fact that the project of rural communitarianism has certain attributes in common with the kind of construction that Neogi was espousing, one can discover some common ground beneath their manner of philosophising and in their notion of ethics. That is why Gandhi and Tagore are important figures in the search for an alternative.

Gandhi, of course, is by far the more significant personality in this context. And this is not just because he was a mass leader of far greater consequence, though this did contribute to the characteristics of Gandhism, which are vital to this search. Ethics, morality, politics, and his epistemology, or search for truth, were all inextricably interwoven into what sometimes appears, to a mind bred on Western modes of argument, to be a hopelessly confused mass.

There are certain fundamental similarities between the

positions of Gandhi and Tagore regarding *Swaraj* (as Gandhi called it) or *Samaj* (as Tagore called it), that is their conception of what constitutes freedom for the masses of India. In the course of elaborating on this, they drew a distinction between **state** and **society**. On the basis of a sweeping summary of the history of the Indian people, from the ancient times to the colonial period, Tagore[7] concluded that the strength of the people of India lay in the independence or self-sufficiency of the village community. This marked them as different from the Western nations in which the people were dependent on the state. We are not concerned with the correctness of this omnibus view of history. (In any case truth, correctness and such else have long been under a huge question mark.[8] We believe that there is much to be said in favour of the position that one writes history in order to persuade others to a particular course of action.) Gandhi said much the same thing[9] as Tagore. Interestingly, the theme of Asiatic Mode of Production, inaugurated by Marx and which has fascinated scores of social scientists through a century, [10] suggests the same difference, but in a pejorative sense. In sum, they all suggested that the rural community in India was more or less self-sufficient, in economic and social-organisational terms. The state and the urban centres, to the extent that they existed, were parasitic. While Tagore and Gandhi lauded this as a sign of strength of the community or society (*Samaj*), Marx denigrated this as being the root cause of a stagnant society and economy. The people were so complacent in their stagnant, idyllic village that conquests by invading armies and consequent change in monarchy hardly bothered them.

In this era of globalisation, this idea of the *Samaj* or the Asiatic community, undisturbed in its economy and society by the rent-appropriating monarch, becomes crucial. As we have argued, this is precisely the relation between global capital and the non-capitalist sector. Contrary to what was believed by orthodox Marxism, capital has no mission to organise all productive activities in the world according to capitalist principles. It makes more profit, and therefore more sense, to keep certain enclaves outside the organisational structure of global capital. These niches can then be used to put out work at low cost. The confined local is a source of rent extraction by global capital.

The movement for *Swaraj* was a movement for reviving the local as a counter-hegemonic position against the global. In the context in which this movement was launched, global was identified with the colonial state, while the local was the village community, which had lost some of its independence during colonial rule. The essence of the movement was to be the social, cultural and economic mobilisation to restore the independence of the *Samaj*. There was an uneasy alliance between the movement for *Swaraj* and the nationalist movement. The reason behind this unease becomes clearer in the current context. To counter the hegemony of global capital, it has become imperative to launch a movement for *Swaraj*, with global networking. It can no longer be confused with any struggle against imperial capital, in the sense of foreign capital. Today the struggle for *Swaraj* has to be a struggle against rent-extracting global capital, irrespective of whether it originates within that nation itself. Partha Chatterjee (Chatterjee, P., 1986) has argued along, what we think are basically Western, Hegelian[11] lines that the communitarianism of Gandhi had a specific role at the moment of history in which it emerged. In Chatterjee's scheme, one would say that the 'moment of manoeuvre'[12] has now become redundant. During the struggle for freedom from British rule, according to Chatterjee's mode of reasoning, it was necessary for Gandhi as a political leader, functioning within a bourgeois legal framework, to construct the highway where *Swaraj* and the aspiration for national freedom within this legal framework could meet and, further, he had himself to manoeuvre along this path. This meeting was never an integral part of Gandhi's thought. The core of the project of Gandhi (and also of Tagore) was dismissive of the state. In the age of globalisation, for all economic intents and purposes, the question of nationalism has degenerated into a bogey raised by segments with vested interest in some kind of pseudo-nationalistic fervour. Today the issue of *Swaraj* has become delinked from nationalist struggle. To be meaningful, in fact this inspirational idea has to spread out to all corners of the globe – the global networking between the local, countering the global power of capital.

The question of the moral and ethical regeneration of those engaged in the movement, which was highlighted often by Guha Neogi, had also been a matter of deep concern to both Tagore and Gandhi. All of them were experimenting with interweaving the construction of the local socio-economic structure with the construction of woman/man-in-society. This was reflected in Chhattisgarh, to give just one example, in the refusal of the workers to accept contributions from outside for the construction of the Shahid Hospital. The principle was that one should not accept outside help for social construction, as far as possible, as this would weaken the resolve of the local against the global. In fact, this objective fundamentally determined the course of all the movements initiated by CMM. This compulsion was also prominent in the many exhortations of Gandhi to the *satyagrahis* as well as in the addresses of Tagore to his countrymen regarding *swadesh* (one's own land) and *samaj*. This idea was encapsulated in their thought in the notion of 'self-respect' and 'self-dependence', to which they gave so much prominence.

There is a profound difference between the attitudes of Tagore and Gandhi, on the one hand, and of Neogi, on the other, regarding extensiveness of the moral and ethical[13] regeneration required. This difference is related with the divergence between their approaches to the question of direct democracy vis-à-vis representative democracy. In proposing a classification of nations based on the relative importance accorded to state and to the community in economic and social affairs, Tagore[14] clearly comes out in support of the Indian system which gives the greatest prominence to the local community, virtually ignoring the parasitic state. He attributes the abject surrender to the British to the abdication of economic and social responsibilities by the community. Consequently, he advocates the revitalisation of the community bonds. Gandhi is scathingly sceptical of the system of representative governance.[15] His faith resides in the village community. To this extent, Neogi has a clear affinity with Tagore, Gandhi and a lot of rural communitarians. But this seems to be the limit of the faith of the communitarians in the community of equal people, during the period of the nationalist struggle. Tagore feels the community can be restored to its pre-eminent position only if a leader emerges, who embodies the virtues of the community. Almost in identical terms Gandhi draws a clear distinction between the common participants in the movement, who are motivated not by truth which has been internalised by them (but by other factors like uncritical faith in nationalism as conveyed to them), and the *Satyagrahis* who lead a truthful life and are motivated by the truth which they experience. The common person is also to be welcomed to the fold of the movement as a follower, though they may be moved by different considerations and their support may even be issue based. The tensions in the positions come through in a lot of areas. Perhaps a bit surprising, it was also a prominent area of disagreement between Gandhi and Tagore. This has been well documented in English by Sabyasachi Bhattacharya (1999).[16]

On the other hand, a key concern of the movement launched by CMSS was that there should exist a continuous effort to democratise the movement. This implied that the principles of a radically democratic society had to be evolved in the course of the effort for its establishment, and these had to be internalised, both in the ethos and culture of those who joined the struggle, as well as in the organisational principles of CMSS.[17] This changes the significance of the boundary between the moral and the ethical as well. Just as the people participating in the movement developed their personal ideas about what was right and wrong in the course of their movement of opposition and construction, social norms were also created. The two emerged entwined, without any need for transition, unlike in the case of the dialectical model of the West in which Tagore had obvious faith.

A Slice of Philosophy

Beyond a point, Gandhi's apparent loss of faith in the community can largely be attributed to his increasing concern with the exigencies of leading mammoth political movements, as has been suggested by Chatterjee (Chatterjee, P., 1986) and others. But, at the same time, one can see an attempt to provide some kind of philosophic justification of a contingent solution along what appears to be distinctly Hegelian lines. Tagore, while advocating the role of the *samajpati* (which translates literally to 'leader of the community) sounds uncannily like a Hegelian, complete with the 'universal – particular' binary (Tagore,1905).

There is actually a displacement of what was also apparently an insurmountable problem for Hegel. Partha Chatterjee has critiqued this aspect of Hegel's Philosophy of Rights (Chatterjee, P., 1994) in the context of establishing the superiority of discursive construction of the society that has community as its elementary aspect or starting point, over one that has self as its elementary aspect. I think Chatterjee's treatment deserves a summary appraisal at this point. This can be a suitable point of departure for evaluating the role assigned to the leader of the community in the writings of Gandhi and Tagore.

Hegel starts his journey from self. Chatterjee faults Hegel for illicitly, and covertly, importing the notion of community (as family) at the moment of transition from morality to ethics. The point is well taken, but this, as I have pointed out elsewhere (Basu, P. K., 2001), is a failure of dialectical construction and not just of Hegel's particular construction. Let us try to understand this lack in this system avoiding the terminological density (that philosophical discourses employ for rigour) to the extent that it jars with the tone and tenor of our discussion.

Suppose one starts the dialectical journey from **oneself**. This self-in-isolation is purely abstract. Or one may say that it has no mooring in, or is totally cut off from, the **external or physical world**. It is just the untamed will of the individual. Then, within this system of logic starts a dialogue or a process of reasoning. The opposite position, or what is called the anti-thesis, to pure and abstract self as the thesis, is that of pure externality. That is, the other initiates the dialogue by saying, 'but your notion cannot take account of the material world, even of your own body. All that is **pure externality'**. Then both come to an understanding or to a synthesis of their initial positions: the external world is connected with the will of self (which is the differentia of pure selfhood) through the notion of property.

The external world becomes the property of self. In other words, **right to property** becomes the connection between self and the external world or the ground on which they meet. Self or will externalises itself by making the external world its property.

The other continues the dialogue, saying, 'Why should the journey start from yourself and not from myself? Then I will have **my property** just as you have **your property'**. They agree and try to find the common ground or meeting place for their separate properties. They find that these properties meet only when they are exchanged. In other words, the two separate properties meet only when the two property holders contract to exchange. So, **contract** becomes the next meeting ground or higher synthesis. It is the essence of property. This means that the specificity of this property or that property is lost in the act of contracting to exchange. You have to continue the dialogue as long as there is any possibility of positing a contradictory view, or the antithesis, to the synthesis that has been reached up to that point. That is as long as, what the philosophers call, the absolute universal or ground on which all positions can stand (as 'particulars' or simply different expressions of the universal or ground) has not been attained.

So the other says, 'So far so good. But what if one of us breaks the contract? That is someone does wrong?' So, **wrong** becomes the antithesis of the **right** to property and contract. Then where do these two meet? Right and wrong can meet (that is, one can be differentiated from the other) only on the ground of morality. When all the different selves *individually, in their own minds (that is subjectively)* develop a sense of what is right and what is wrong. This subjective sense is precisely what is called **morality**. The problem occurs at this juncture.

The notion of social unity on the ground of morality is only subjective. We may all have different notions of what is a moral action, of what should constitute a defensible right to property. For example, as we have argued in the course of discussing the morality of construction of big dams, there could be differences of opinions regarding the relative merit of recognising the ancient common rights of the forest-dependent people on natural resources, and of disregarding these rights in favour of rights which are consistent with the process of 'modernising' through mega projects. Overcoming the subjectivity of morality for the construction of a 'universal' **ethics** is neither a logical nor an irreversible process. So the mechanism of this transition cannot be captured within the frame of dialectics. An NBA activist, and those dwelling in the catchment area would subscribe to a morality, which upholds the traditional rights of the forest dweller; the sugar plant owner, the urban dweller, the modernising economist would all favour a morality that bestows the right on the user who utilises this in a way which the market principle, buttressed by some shoddy principle of 'notional compensation'[18], judges to be more efficient. The dialogue, therefore, cannot continue beyond this point. It is displaced into a power struggle, where the weaker is obviously the loser.

Hegel, the modern *guru* of the dialectical system (that is, reasoning through the kind of dialogue we have just cited) uses a sleight of hand at this point, which Chatterjee rightly criticises. Hegel imports community organisations like the family and the school, which bring up the child in such a way that he/she imbibes the universal ethics of the community. This, however, begs the question of construction of the universal. Who or what is to decide which should be the 'proper' ethics? In our scheme this is *the* field of power struggle, of primitive capital accumulation (in a particular context). It was the power of global capital that decided the contest between the ethics of the tribals inhabiting the mountain forests that were inundated by the waters of Sardar Sarovar and the ethics of the sugar cane growers and urban electricity consumers who gained from the construction of the dam.

The general problem is the inability of the dialectical system to theorise transition or any kind of voluntary action. Such actions are only seen as aberrations, which are like random movements round a fated, dialectical, teleological course that is inevitably evolutionary (that is breaks or jumps – in logic as much as in history – have to be glossed over). Chatterjee does not see this as a failure of the method itself and locates the illogic at the level of the particular historical journey that Hegel is narrating. Predictably, he too falls into this trap. Chatterjee's re-enactment of the fall[19] is not important for our purpose. What is important, however, is why dialectical logic fails at this juncture.

The reason, as we have already mentioned in passing, is the inability of the dialectical system of Hegel to take account of purposive action. Purposive construction, which is simultaneously moral and ethical (or where the difference is always necessarily seeking solution in 'practice') bridges this gap – the transition from morality to ethics. The projects of social construction that were undertaken by CMM, KSSP and various Gandhian organisations may be mentioned. In a sense the dialectical method of Hegel presumes that any observed object or field of enquiry has an essential core. This may also be called the truth of the object. To paraphrase Hegel, the rest is dross that can be separated from the true kernel by dialectical enquiry. There is therefore an absolute ethics waiting to be uncovered. This is unchanging. When this has been dug out by means of dialectical enquiry, and codified in society, the subjective morality of individuals will also coincide with this absolutely true ethics. Ethics and morality will lose their distinction. The method of *Nirman aur Sangharsh* (construction and struggle), on the other hand, does not subscribe to any idea of a given and constant *true ethics* waiting to be discovered. Through this rejection, the idea that there is an end of history is also banished. Since there is no true essence of social order, there is no question of this truth's being manifested at the end of history. There is therefore no teleology either. The process of construction creates, simultaneously, the ethics and morality of the future, which is also always evolving.

Let us stop awhile. Look at what we called the hyperreality of the global order that we inhabit. The ethics is the ethics of the market and the morality is the consumerist attitude. The individual as consumer is a particular of the universal market. You can complete the circuit of any interpersonal relation only through the market. There is therefore no contradiction between the ethics of the society and morality of the individual. In the course of 'construction and struggle', the difference continues to exist (it is continuously excited and simultaneously threatened – that is the result of the democratic participatory decision making process) and it is this difference and the force that it generates that pushes the movement forward.

The strategy of 'struggle and construct' implies an ethical entry point to the understanding of society. Further, what differentiates this position from the dialectical idealism of Western thought is that the entry point to understanding is also simultaneously the entry point to practice. Practice, as envisioned by CMM, has a subjective element, that is it is inseparable from the question of morality of the individual involved in the practice. This point requires some elaboration. We are not claiming that practice always brings in its train the question of morality of the participants in the practice. Mostly it does not require that the practitioner confront the ethics of the practice or movement with his/her subjective morality. Consider the worker in the factory. His labour time is alienated from him. He has no control over what is done with that time. In plain terms, what this means is that the worker does not decide what sort of productive activity he/she is engaged in. Similarly, the cadre belonging to a disciplined centralised political party simply does the bidding of the party bosses, just as the worker carries out the dictates of the manager. This is true, whether the party professes a left or a right ideology. The question of democracy within the movement becomes important in this context. It is only when the movement allows continuous criticism and self-criticism at every echelon of the organisation that there is an intertwining of the moral with the ethical. Thus this approach implies the absence of the distance between morality and ethics. More correctly, one should say that the distance is itself an object of practice. So again we have the absence of any logical guarantee. It is not as if a particular vision of movement has logically closed what appeared to be an unbridgeable distance between ethics and morality. If this were possible, the problem would have been just a philosophical problem. There has to be a continuous struggle to question private morality with community ethics and to question ethics with morality. To repeat a point that we have been making throughout, the struggle was not only in the socio-political space but simultaneously in the mind. This idea was central in both the movement for health and education.

While it is necessary to understand that theorising cannot be the solution to the problem of lack of correspondence between ethics and morality, it is also necessary to elaborate theoretically on the reason why the practice CMM or of CMSS created a space (within theory) where this transition – from morality to ethics and back – could be thought. In this elaboration, two specific attributes of these movements appear to be important. First, the simultaneity of construction and of struggle: the act of construction will bring to the forefront the tensions and conflicts within the community. For construction to be feasible, it is essential that these conflicts be resolved. So the space of dialogue between the members of the community has to be constructed out of sheer necessity. Second, the emphasis on direct democracy and the opposition to leadership from outside: this immediately creates a field in an in-between space (situated half-way between the subjectivity of the actors and the notion of the integrated community demand for action) where ethics and morality interact.

There was a similar possibility in the approach of the rural communitarians. But this was stifled by the lack of faith of the communitarians in the masses, reflected in their insistence on the crucial role of a mediator. Particularly the idea of *Satyagraha*, propounded by Gandhi, had great potential to bridge the gap between the ethical and the moral standpoint. To the extent that Gandhi relied on the role of the *Satygrahis* in mobilising the masses, his position can be imagined to be a step closer to ours'. But there always remained the possibility of subversion of the ethics of the movement by because of the assigned *instrumental* nature of relation between the Satyagrahis and the masses.

It is precisely at this point of transition from morality to ethics, that Tagore and Gandhi abandon their quest for the moral regeneration of the masses. The ethics is known as if by revelation to the *samajpati*, in the case of Tagore. In Gandhi's frame, there is at least an intermediate layer between the common participants in the nationalist struggle (who are unaware of the ethics) and the benevolent king – the *satygrahis*. They evolve and imbibe the ethics in the course of their truthful and non-violent struggle. By positing the benevolent despot, Tagore erases the problem of how the common person is to imbibe the ethics proper to the *samaj*. Again one may suggest that this difference followed from the differences in the practical compulsions of their respective positions. While Gandhi had to mobilise a large body of protesters to effectively confront the colonial state non-violently, Tagore had no such direct political obligation. He could, therefore afford to leave the question of ethics to the administration of the benevolent despot; while Gandhi had to ensure that the ethic of *Swaraj* was not 'polluted' by the political practice of the nationalist struggle. In any case, they both foreclose the question of internalising of the community ethics by all the members of the community.

Differences: Neogi and the Communitarians

The two fundamental areas of difference between the ideas of CMM and those of Tagore and Gandhi centre on the questions of direct democracy versus despotic rule and of rights. The differences as well as the significance of these differences are best elaborated using the insights of the post-modern Marxists, or the Althusserians.

We start from rights – rights particularly to the surplus produced within a social order. This issue is strikingly absent in the writings of the rural communitarians. To the rural communitarians, social ethics was all. This was part of the *samaj* and did not require to be buttressed by the coercive authority of the state. This was broadly the position that was articulated by Chatterjee, to whom we have already referred (Chatterjee, P., 1994). Once the self-evolving universal dharma, based on the equality of castes, is in place, the source of social conflict vanishes. The great divide between the Western nations, where civil society was based on the legal framework erected by the state, and the Eastern nations, whose society was relatively independent, exercised its own seduction. Deifying the self-sufficiency of the Indian rural community vis-à-vis the state, Tagore, Gandhi and the others of this genre wish away the question of power, together with the state. Just as state is posited as an outsider, the power to appropriate surplus also becomes an issue, which is not internal to the rural community. Hence it does not merit any separate consideration – it would vanish with the regeneration of society and the consequent severance of its ties with the state.

A typical orthodox Marxist response would be to say that this was part of the conspiracy of the domestic ruling classes to hide their exploitative character. Given the economic position of communitarians, like Tagore and Gandhi, it is a relatively simple task for one subscribing to economic determinism (as orthodox Marxists do), to attribute the neglect of the question of power and of unequal rights within the rural economy to the vested interests of these communitarians. But one of the positive contributions of post-modernism to our way of thinking is that it has reasserted, in a convincing way, the poverty of thought which ascribes all our actions to some single aspect of our being. Suffice it to comment, in passing, that it is thoroughly churlish and most unconvincing to claim that Tagore and even more so, Gandhi, was thinking of the interests of the elite, in contrast to our Marxist leaders who think continuously of the working class, and of it alone. The genesis of the problem can perhaps be traced to the way in which these communitarians looked at the question of power and its relation to the state. They contextualised these questions within the field of politics. A similar problem plagues the works of a lot of historians, like Chatterjee. Their eschewal of the economic determinism, which characterised the works of the early Marxist and nationalist historians writing about the economy, has provided invaluable insights about the way in which economic decision making is influenced by social, cultural and other factors. But, at the same time, there is a tendency to denigrate the role of the economy, to the detriment of a proper understanding of the dynamics of the social system. Looked at from this perspective, the elusive problem is assigning proper weight to one level of social intercourse, without diminishing the importance of another level of interaction. The Althusserians of the *Rethinking Marxism* group have made a seminal contribution to the unravelling of this problem through their elaboration of the Althusserian concept of overdetermination. We have introduced this idea in our introductory chapter.

The various levels of social interaction intermingle and penetrate all social activity. To make sense of this complex totality, we have to approach 'reality' from our own chosen[20] perspective. This has been constituted by our image of what society ought to be. Our focus has been on the question of appropriation and distribution of surplus of material production. From this angle, whenever surplus is produced, the fundamental question is the right to this surplus. It is possible that there is a geographical separation between the producer and appropriator of surplus, as happens in the case of the Asiatic Mode of Production. This has certain similarities with the position of the communitarians, as pointed out earlier. But even for this system to work it is necessary that the distant appropriator of surplus has the power to define the rights within the surplus-producing system so as to be able to be able to appropriate surplus.

The lack of faith in the ability of the community to directly decide its own ethics, as well as the absence of any special privilege for the working class in the frame of thought of the rural communitarians (and historians, like Chatterjee) stems from the neglect of the economic level of social activity. If this level of activity is considered, then the question of production comes to the fore. The class (or classes) of surplus appropriators then comes (come) out as a strong impediment to the formation of a community ethics. One has then to give prominence to the working class in the struggle for the new ethics. Further, the very existence of surplus in any social formation points to the persistent possibility of conflict over this surplus. Hence direct and continuous participation of the members of the community in the evolution of the community ethics becomes an absolute necessity.

A specificity of discourse on the economic is that, unlike the discourses on the other levels of social interaction, the object of deployment of economic power (i.e. surplus production and appropriation) is defined independently of the power itself. So, this discourse can accommodate the continued existence of the object of power beyond the age of that specific power. In discourse about the other kinds of social interaction, the object of power and the power itself are defined conterminously.

Let us elaborate on this point. We take off from our sketchy introduction to the structural linguistics of Saussure (note 6, p. 98). We had said that, according to this view, reality is never accessible in our thought. But we can still make sense because there is a definite connection between the linguistic representation (called the *signifier*) and the image that it conjures (called the *signified*). But post-structuralism goes beyond this. It argues that there is no stability of the relation between a signifier and a signified. This happens precisely because of the inaccessibility of the real or *referential* world in our thought. Simplistically, one could put it thus. Because of this lack of access, there is a constant sliding of the signifieds along the surface of a signifier. There is no constancy of the relation. Another is continuously replacing one meaning. For example, the term 'value' or 'valuable' means different things to different people and to the same person in different contexts. Then we do not even have the comfort of the little sense that structural linguistics promised. How then do we remain intelligible to ourselves and to others? Here some others (Laclau, E. and – Mouffe, C., 2001) introduce the concept of a master signifier to show how we make sense. The master signifier (also called the nodal point) in a particular context is a word-concept that imparts meaning to all other words in a broad, related field. For example, 'market price' is such a master signifier. It imparts meanings to 'value', 'efficiency', even 'good' and so on. We are now equipped somewhat to understand what we mean by the statement that in social interaction, other than in the field of economic, the object of power and the power itself are defined coterminously.

Within bourgeois culture the most prominent master signifier is market price. This is what imparts sense to all discourses about culture, ethics, and so on. The rural communitarians, in their writings about the ought of the cultural milieu, were acutely critical of this market culture. What they wanted instead was to establish community-sanctioned need as the master signifier. The power of bourgeois culture was exercised through the dominance of market price as the master signifier. The struggle for the mind was the struggle to replace this with another – in this case community need – master signifier. The object of struggle was the master signifier itself.

Thus evolution of a communitarian ethics is the end of the story as far as, say, discussion on the polity is concerned. But, the transition to a local community-based economic order does not imply a solution of the problem of appropriation and distribution of surplus, which is the fundamental object of economic power. If a growing economy has to be sustained, it has to produce a surplus. So the ethics have to be continuously evolved through the direct participation of all the working people in the construction of the community, which itself is always being reconstructed.

When we look at this economic dimension of the social order, much of the confusions get clarified. An economy that does not produce surplus is, at best, a stagnant economy. Actually, it is a dying economy assuming that population is increasing. So the question of power remains central to any egalitarian project. Once surplus is produced, the economy cannot be ordered simply by the principle of equality. One may, for example, think of a need-based equality. The output of the society is distributed according to the socially sanctioned needs. Individual needs differ. So output is not distributed equally in a quantitative sense. As Ajit Chaudhury has elaborated in his seminal contribution to the discussion of economic equality,[21] equality can only be established in a qualitative sense. And this will always involve quantitative inequality. The intensity of labour varies between activities. So the needs are different. The needs of a mineworker will, obviously, be greater than that of a teacher. If society does not recognise this but gives them equally, this would not lead to equality. The necessary or subsistence production is distributed unequally, in a quantitative sense, to generate equality. All accept this. But they have no reason to support the same unequal distribution of surplus in a society based on equality. So conflict arises. The communitarian society of Tagore and Gandhi, as well as the village community in the Asiatic Mode of Production resolve this problem by simply giving up the surplus to an outsider – the state. But once the outside ceases to exist, once *Swaraj* has been attained, the outside appropriator will have ceased to exist. So the society will have to evolve and elaborate its concept of rights, which cannot be based merely on the principle of equality.

Cooperation is not just about ethics and cultural values. It is essential to evolve a structure of rights proper to the communitarian intention. Ethics, morality, and rights – all buttress each other to create the community's structure. This structure evolves in the course of the struggle to construct. And because the question of rights is inseparably linked to this constructive project, conflict with the given structure of rights, so with the state is inevitable. This is not to diminish, in any way, the significance of the struggle on the cultural front. But it does highlight the problem of erasure of the economic in the frame of discussion of the communitarians.

This also connects with the question of direct versus indirect democracy. Neogi always insisted on direct democracy, while Tagore and Gandhi were often content to leave things to some one or more individuals who embodied the principles of community equality. Neogi insisted on direct democracy as far as practicable. Of course, one must add the rider that the communitarians were also insistent about the need for Panchayati Raj institutions. Unless the producers of surplus, associated in some form of cooperative, directly decide the use of the surplus output, there is always the threat of some individual or group arrogating to itself the authority of utilising the surplus in the name of the community. This, in a sense, amounts to the right of appropriation of surplus. The history of the failure of socialist struggles is strewn with examples of such good intentions gone awry. Once we appreciate the significance of the economic dimension of society and of production of surplus, we can understand the importance of the question of rights and of the form of political organisation of society. It is because the economic dimension, particularly the significance of production of surplus, is not given any importance by them, that the communitarians fall into the idealist trap of reducing the entire question of constructing the new *Samaj* to the ethical level of evolving the universal *Dharma*. Neogi, while imbibing a lot from Gandhi, in particular, always had the economic dimension in mind. Perhaps this can be attributed to his trade union association. Trade union was always his dominant concern.

The question of direct democracy is also important in the course of constructive movements. Neogi, following in the footsteps of the rural communitarians, did not believe in the postponement of the constructive project till after the transformation of the state. In fact, just as the latter, he believed that unless the significance of cooperative construction was realised, struggle would degenerate into a petty game of dislodging one entrenched state power with another. The question of redefining power cannot be framed without the active component of community construction. So, both the element of direct or participatory decision making and the element of constructive practice are epistemologically significant also. It is only through the direct experience of planning distribution and expansion within the ambit of the community that one can visualise the alternative to the power of subjugation that seems to be unavoidable.

An Overview

Contrary to the wisdom of the dominant economic theory (i.e. neoclassical theory) globalisation is not about ensuring coordination of economic activities according to the rationality of the market, the world over. It is not about ensuring that impediments to the freedom of the market be removed. Indeed, the idea that the economy can function according to the non-discriminatory, most efficient and self-sufficient logic of the market is a myth that has been assiduously cultivated by the ruling economic order.

Market itself is unavoidably based on laws and regulations which in themselves and in the process of their coming into being, are no less predatory than the coercive system prevalent within other orders, which are generally accepted to be based on force of arms (in contrast to the capitalist system that is supposedly organised on the principle of equal rights). These rules, laws and regulations are established by force through a process that has been termed as Primitive Capital Accumulation. This process establishes a specific set of discriminatory rights, which are then used to extract rent. As these rights are created, other rights are abrogated. Further, the same process fixes the limits of mobility of resources, including labour and produced goods. Immobility, together with the specific discriminatory rights of the marketplace, generates rent for the right holders. Understandably, the interests of the segments of capital that are more powerful decide the limits of mobility.

The process of PCA benefits some – those who are enabled to extract rent as a result of this process. It also works to the detriment of a much larger segment – those who are deprived of their 'traditional' rights. This clash of interests and the consequent need for force to decide the issue has two important implications, which we have highlighted. First, state power has to act on behalf of capital to facilitate PCA. Second, violence being contingent and its outcome not fully predictable, there is always indeterminacy within the system. The uncertainty and risk are not always, or even preferably, closed with the help of state violence. Hence arises the need for negotiation, bargaining and so on. *When capital complains about the muscle power of Trade Unions, for example, it is actually piqued that its muscle power is being challenged. It is not as if, markets work logically without the intervention of force.*

Our analysis of globalisation led to the conclusion that globalisation is fundamentally the process of distorting rights and forcibly circumscribing mobility of a vast range of productive resources, including labour and knowledge as also of produced goods, so as to enable *global capital* to extract rent, the world over. Force brings in its train the need for state violence. Hence, the dependence of global capital on the imperial states to further its interests around the globe. Since capital is global in its sourcing and reach, there is no necessary correspondence between the worldwide domination by global capital and the imperial power of any particular nation state. This is a conjunctural outcome that is the result of the past history of imperialism. It is conceivable that some time in the future, patriotic economists and politicians will be able to proudly march in support of the Indian army occupying some country to uphold 'liberty' or whatever.

Put pithily, globalisation is therefore the worldwide violent campaign to further the economic interests of the globally mobile at the cost of the local. Wouldn't the appropriate counter hegemonic strategy be to insist on allowing mobility to all? That, as we have argued, is not an option. For one thing, absolute mobility leads to perfect homogenisation, wiping out the local and locality. The local is concrete, embedded in the regional culture and environment. Absolute mobility for all, even if feasible, will lead to the loss of both cultural and environmental diversity. For another, it is not possible to move all resources – some, like land and river are physically confined.

The counter-hegemonic position does not hark back to a pristine past. In fact, the definition of the 'local' needs to be worked out by victims of globalisation in the course of their struggle. Hence we argued for a process of struggle and construct. It is only through a struggle that is involved in local production can one articulate the meaning of what constitutes the local at the present time – its needs and aspirations. *It should be obvious that though some of the elementary aspects of this counter hegemonic struggle can be highlighted through the critique of globalisation, as we have attempted, to work out a blueprint would violate our basic arguments*. The counter-hegemonic position cannot be worked out the basis of abstract reasoning, which is all that we are indulging in: the difference of the local from global is that while global is grounded on the notion of homogeneity, local is based on the notion of concrete and heterogeneous. So much for some preliminary discussion on the elementary aspects of a counter-hegemonic practice in the age of globalisation. We have already stuck out our neck much further than we had bargained for!

NOTES

1. Obviously we are talking of the left movement outside what used to be called or is still called the socialist world. That is not to

suggest that the left movement in these countries have shown consistently greater imagination. But the reason for omitting any discussion about them is that failure of the left in these countries to sustain the dream requires separate enquiry.

2. Roughly the arena where the actors who perceive themselves as equal citizens act out their lives, performing economic, cultural, religious and other functions which are deemed to belong to the private domain by bourgeois culture.
3. Saussure had argued that reality is not accessible in thought. Our thought is necessarily infected by the limitations of symbolic representation. Saussure did not differentiate between the different systems of representation in the context of the power to access reality. In Saussure's scheme inaccessibility of the real is not an empirical problem depending on the conjunctural or accidental characteristics of some systems of representation. It is the result of the philosophical restrictions of representation as such. In contrast Charles Pierce had argued that the degree of accessibility of reality in a system of representation depends on the specific nature of the system of representation. (Footnote 36). Baudrillard can be argued to take off from this point. It is the characteristic of the present age of capital that reality has been rendered absolutely inaccessible.

   "Such a schematization bears some similarity to that of the postmodernist Jean Baudrillard. Baudrillard interprets many representations as a means of concealing the absence of reality; he calls such representations 'simulacra' (or copies without originals) (Baudrillard, 1984). He sees a degenerative evolution in modes of representation in which signs are increasingly empty of meaning: These would be the successive phases of the image:
   1. It is the reflection of a basic reality.
   2. It masks and perverts a basic reality.
   3. It masks the *absence* of a basic reality.
   4. It bears no relation to any reality whatever: it is its own simulacrum." Baudrillard quoted in (Chandler, net.)

   That is the present is not only marked by the total inaccessibility of reality in our thought, but we are not even haunted by this problem. The symbolic space – of the market, primarily – constructs an as if reality, a hyperreality in our minds. It is this that we are content to inhabit. The use to which we can put a commodity does not determine our demand for it; it is the lifestyle that the ads promise to the users, to take a rather banal example. To continue with our banality, it is the use that is liable to interpretation, and opens up to imagination. This is precisely what is denied in the hyperreal space that we inhabit. The force fields of Lacan that we had referred to in footnote 38 are the imaginary, the real and the symbolic (Evans, 1966). Hyperreality has erased both 'reality' and 'imaginary'.

4. The situationist critique of capitalism is modernized in that it integrates the effects of mass media on the minds and behaviour of the workers in contemporary consumer culture. The Situationist International advocated the voluntary & spontaneous creation of *workers councils* at the time of a worker's revolution which would democratically own and manage the means of capital production, in order to ensure equal distribution of wealth: from each according to their ability, to each according to their needs. Most vital to situationists was the avoidance of any reliance on a set of bureaucratic administrators, but rather the creation of a grass-roots, bottom-up democratic structure, with maximal preservation of liberty for the individual. Obviously, by definition, the Situationist International was a revolutionary, dissident movement... far to the left of what was considered the official "left".
5. Among academics Mao was never accorded the recognition that was due to his philosophy and mode of philosophising perhaps the lone exception being Althusser. Now of course his name has unfortunately become identified with 'revolutionary' terrorism (if the two can go together!) because of the political practise of groups who proclaim their allegiance to his thoughts. There are so many writings by Mao on the theme we are on that it is impossible to cite them in a single footnote. It is also the difficult to interpret his ideas pithily because of the poetic mellifluousness of his writings. There is one piece however where, to my mind, the ideas that we are referring to here come through very starkly. It is in his talk on democratic centralism (Mao, 1962).
6. B.N.Ganguly (1977, chapter 4) offers a helpful overview of the early roots of this idea in India
7. Tagore, 1905.
8. That is ever since the postmodernists have begun to question whether concepts like truth and origin are not themselves ideological constructs meant to serve certain power positions. Consider, for example, the significance of the term "original" when one says, "the original noble prize that was given to Tagore has been stolen". What is the medallion? It is a mark signifying that the poet was recognised as a noble laureate. Whenever we

say this we replicate this mark. There is nothing more or less significant about this mark as compared with the "original" mark. The originality of the medallion had to be constructed and sanctified by the authorities of Visva-Bharati in order to add to their power as the main repository of Tagore's earthly bequests. Of course, this has now enhanced the value derived by the thief!

The post-modernists say that the so-called original is not intimated to us, as such, through any non-representational communication. It is known and communicated in and through a system of representation, generally linguistic. That the village community was the original form of social association in India is also an impression generated in our minds by an accumulation of marks or signs which indicate this "originality"(one of these is that Tagore said so!).

9. Gandhi, 1910.
10. A flavour of the kind of work this has excited can be had from Bailey and Llobera, 1981.
11. Georg Wilhelm Friedrich Hegel (1770 – 1831), was a German philosopher best known for popularizing the dialectical method of reasoning. Hegel's dialectic, which he usually presented in a threefold manner, was vulgarized by Heinrich Moritz Chalybäus as comprising three dialectical stages of development: a thesis, giving rise to its reaction, an antithesis which contradicts or negates the thesis, and the tension between the two being resolved by means of a synthesis. Hegel rarely used these terms himself: this model is not Hegelian but Fichtean.

    In the **Logic**, for instance, Hegel describes a dialectic of existence: first, existence must be posited as pure Being; but pure Being, upon examination, is found to be indistinguishable from Nothing. When it is realized that what is coming into being is, at the same time, also returning to nothing (consider life: old organisms die as new organisms are created or born), both Being and Nothing are united as Becoming.

    As in the Socratic dialectic, Hegel claimed to proceed by making implicit contradictions explicit: each stage of the process is the product of contradictions inherent or implicit in the preceding stage. For Hegel, the whole of history is one tremendous dialectic, major stages of which chart a progression from self- alienation as slavery to self-unification and realization as the rational, constitutional state of free and equal citizens.
12. The idea of manoeuvre is derived from Gramsci.
13. Perhaps a clarification is necessary. We are using the terms

'ethical' and 'moral' as used within a specific discourse where their difference rather than their substitutability is important – the Hegelian discourse. 'Moral' refers to the individual's subjective notion of right and wrong. 'Ethical' refers to the socially accepted norms of right and wrong.

14. Tagore, 1905
15. Gandhi, 1910
16. The discord related to differences of attitude towards the non-cooperation movement between 1919 and 1922. Tagore was of the view that *Satyagraha* should not be used as a tactics of struggle but that it should be above all a means to reflect and internalise the ethics on which the future *Swadeshi samaj* was to be built. Unless this was possible he was of the opinion that the movement should be abandoned as it could lead the movement away from its chosen path of truth. Gandhi understandably took a more pragmatic view because he had to organise a movement against the existing imperial order.
17. This ethos was a significant component of Mao's thoughts as pointed out in note 5 of this chapter.
18. The prevailing orthodoxy in economic theory pretends to be able to do without any value judgement. It claims that such 'interpersonal comparisons' are best left to the politicians while the economists get on with scientific evaluation of alternative policies. Adopting any set of policies in preference to another must involve loss to some and gain to some others. How then can one make policy decisions without interpersonal comparisons? The rather ingenuous answer is provided by the principle of 'notional compensation'. As long as the sugarcane growers, the electricity consumers, and all others who gain from Sardar Sarovar make a total gain whose monetary value is more than that of the total losses incurred by those displaced by the project, the project would be justified, according to the logic of the ruling economic theory. Whether the losers are actually compensated by the transference of some of the gains of the gainers is immaterial. As long as it is possible to compensate the losers then the project is deemed to be desirable. The dirty business of actual payment (or non-payment) of compensation is the concern of the politician. The economist, for the purpose of his calculation, assumes that the compensation has been made. This is called notional compensation.

    But the sleight is not confined to the deferment of the act of compensation to the realm of the political. The very idea that there can be a quantitative comparison of the gains and losses involves a suppression of the subordinated cultural values of the potential oustees – to those displaced by the construction of the dam the loss of their way of life has no monetary equivalent.

19. Chatterjee thinks, quite without basis, that if the narration had started from the community as the elementary presupposition or agency, rather than the individual, then this problem would not have arisen. The community, which can inculcate ethical values is, after all, already in place and so does not have to be illegally imported as in Hegel's case. What Chatterjee does not realise is that the problem is simply displaced from the terrain of the community to the terrain of the community of communities. That is, to the terrain of the universal community from which the particular communities derive their meaning. As I have argued in my PhD thesis, there is no reason for the members of a particular caste to subjectively generate (that is within and through just a dialogue with the other castes) the universal *dharma* (religion) of equal castes. If this is a logical possibility, then there should be no problem either with the transition from morality to ethics in the Hegelian frame. To pursue the parallel: the individual *dharma* of each caste can be considered to be the metaphor of morality and the universal *dharma* that Chatterjee posits as a possibility can be considered as the metaphor of ethics.
20. The choice of word is perhaps inappropriate. We are not talking of choice in a purely subjective way. Indeed, given a postmodern position one cannot have a pure, single or essential determinant of any action.
21. Ajit Chaudhury, 1992.

10

Situating the Position

I have said what I set out to. What remains is, in a way, not substantive, that is if one is willing to leave questions of theory aside. But a point that we have been trying to hammer home is that all descriptions of social structures (and even 'scientific observations') are influenced by the point of view of the narrator or the theory on which the narration is based. A major casualty of capitalist globalisation is critical thought. Operational analysis and positivist thought rule the roost. We hardly stop to think how our thoughts are thought for us. A major motivation behind the book is to incite the reader to think critically. It is imperative, therefore that the reader evaluates the theoretical background of our narrative of the current reality.

Those readers who have some familiarity with the broadly leftist literature on political economy of development may be wondering already where we are situated. This chapter marks our distances from some of the kindred efforts. Throughout the preceding chapters, I have concentrated on defining my views on the global economy through a critique of the ruling neoclassical theory. As we mentioned in the first chapter, most of the left positions, in contrast to our approach, are argued through critiques of other left positions. We have consciously eschewed this path. In spite of sharp disagreements with many 'left' positions, we feel that the greater ideological impediments (within the domain of economic thought) to the construction of a more humane global ethos and to people's movements to thwart the aggrandising journey of global capital are still the various neoclassical or bourgeois economic apologies of globalisation. We have therefore tried to present every facet of our position through critiques of the corresponding apologies offered by neoclassical economics. (In particular cases or expositions of particular events, where we have thought that the ideological battle in defence of global capital is being waged more efficiently by some variant of leftism – as in the case of the eviction of peasants for the procurement of land for industries in the left-ruled state of West Bengal – we have followed the standard leftist practice of defining a position in opposition to other professed left positions.) This was the method of presentation. In my method of analysis, of course, I developed my insights through the articulation of differences with other Marxist positions. This was inevitable, given that the fundamental category of analysis that has shaped our views is 'class'. Though we have discussed questions of power and domination, the criterion that we have used to differentiate segments of the population is who generates surplus and who appropriates it. The question of exploitation is the core of our discussion, unlike in many discussions – some of which we will presently comment upon – that use unspecific criteria, like domination, subjugation, etc. as the central idea. It is not that the approach adopted here gives a clearer or truer view of social reality; only this is the appropriate point of view if the concern is with eliminating exploitation. This is, or should be, the approach that distinguishes any social analysis that claims to be Marxist in lineage from other analyses of society.

In this concluding chapter, we will spell out some of our consonances and disagreements with other 'likeminded' (to deliberately use a vague category) critiques of the current global order. In a sense we will try to elaborate our method of enquiry through contrast. There is a vast literature, which qualifies for consideration. We have considered only some of those contributions, which deal with a problem area that is close to ours – the problem of understanding globalisation. This is not meant to be some sort of survey of literature. The purpose of this chapter, like that of the other chapters is to bring the contours of our approach into sharper focus. Only, we are doing it in a different way in this chapter. Focusing through differentiation is an accepted method of exposition, whose theoretical basis has been firmly established ever since structuralism taught us that meanings exist only in difference.

There is a way of looking at globalisation and its alternatives that has (or had in recent times) gained considerable currency and which, on the surface, appears to be quite contrary to our view of globalisation. This is the view propagated by Hardt, M and Negri, A., 2000 (whom we will henceforth refer to as H&N (2000)). H&N (2000) argue that what we have today is an empire without an imperial nation. It is similar to the great ancient empires in its inclusive expansion. Apparently, these empires had expanded through conquest, but at the same time had included the subjugated within its cultural domain. In a similar move, global capital is expanding its economic domain all over the world and simultaneously bringing the entire world under the sway of its homogenising culture, juridical categories and codes of interaction. Like the ancient empires, it is even fighting the so-called 'just wars' to this end.

Globalisation of capital has severed the dependence of capital on the nation state of origin. In fact, origin has become quite inconsequential. What global capital intends (and largely achieves) is to impose its code of governance and law all over the world. It does not, therefore, make sense to invoke the nation state in the struggle against the new empire: nation states do not face off in the course of the expansionary drive of global capital. So far I would largely concur. I have some differences that are apparently not consequential but which become significant in the context of the broader scheme. For example, as we have represented the global scene, nation states constitute the central agency that imposes the code that is necessary for global capital. Neither is the code universal in the sense of internalised ethics (leaving aside the question of sustainability of such essentialist epistemology). So, force is essential to the project of the new empire. This organised violence is institutionalised through the nation states. Barring a few recalcitrants, nation states – that are all subservient to the dictates of global capital – are organised in a hierarchical military order, which is, to a great extent, contingently determined by the neo-imperialist order of the previous era of imperialism. We have already seen this mechanism at work. In a related sense, imperialism is also influenced by the geographical origins of global capital and the chronological order in which states were sensitised to the needs of this capital. In spite of such differences, I would agree that nation states are no longer the appropriate agency for contesting the 'empire' of global capital, for the obvious reason that they have no independent sovereign national motivation: their policy objectives are generally bounded by the needs of global capital.

My basic disagreement is with the proposal of counter-hegemonic strategy and tactics by H&N. (They do not differentiate between the two, claiming, for reasons that are not of interest to us, that in this age and time the distinction has become irrelevant.) They do not clearly spell out the positive aspects of counter-hegemonic practice, but define these in their differences from other strategies and tactics suggested by the left. They are very specific that counter hegemony cannot be based on struggles that valorise the local as opposed to the global, at least when they introduce their position. In this sense their inclination is, or so it appears at the beginning of their odyssey, in a direction diametrically opposite to ours.

> 'In the long decades of the current crisis of the communist, socialist, and liberal Left that has followed the 1960s, a large portion of critical thought, both in the dominant countries of the capitalist development and in the subordinate ones, has sought to recompose sites of resistance that are founded on the identities of social subjects or national and regional groups, often grounding political analysis on the *localization of struggles*.... Today the operative syllogism at the heart of the various forms of "local" Leftist strategy seems to be entirely reactive: If capitalist domination is becoming ever more global, then our resistance to it must defend the local and construct barriers to capital's accelerating flows...
>
> ...Today this localist position is both false and damaging.... It is false because first, the problem is poorly posed... it rests on a false dichotomy between the global and the local, assuming the

global entails homogenisation and undifferentiated identity, whereas local preserves heterogeneity and difference.' (H&N, 2000: 62)

H&N further extend their argument to claim that the sponsors of locality-based movements forget that the local is as much a discursive ploy as the global and both work within the hegemonic space of global capital.

I quite agree with a number of cautions that they add regarding the pitfalls of locality-based movements. It is also necessary to keep in mind that there may be a tendency to valorise locality as a pre-cultural, originary category. For our part, we have been critically conscious about these and other possible pitfalls, quite without the admonitions of these two authors, as should be evident to the readers who have covered the rest of the book. Particularly, we have repeatedly emphasised that the community that we are talking about is not some pure community that predates capital's onslaught, but a new community of the working people that has to be developed through the process of construction and struggle – *Nirman aur Sangharsh.*

The authors do not base their criticism of 'other Leftist' positions nor the exposition of their own position on any articulated set of theoretical concepts. The only theoretical basis that they offer is a reading of Foucault's notion of differences between hegemonic orders. Specifically, they refer to Foucault's distinction between disciplinary society and the society of control. They characterise the present phase of capital as belonging to the society of control. They use the term 'biopolitical' power – taking off explicitly from Foucault's conception of the capillaries of power and the politics of the body – to depict the nature of hegemony in the society of control. While not denigrating Foucault's contribution to the mechanism of power, I would still suggest that the theoretical basis of his analysis is rather too catholic, and further, when others borrow his terminology and his mode of arguments, they frequently fail to construct the mesh that binds the theoretical concepts together. This is a problem of using Foucault's analytical structure, which is perhaps caused by the fact that Foucault presents applications of rather tense theoretical ideas that are not always articulated theoretically by him. To make a rather hurried remark: if you talk of an all-encompassing power that is not analysed, then counter-hegemonic practice must also be formulated in a vague negative way. It must itself belong to the unanalysed whole,[1] that is it must also be a global practice. From this follows the authors' impatience with the localised strategies of counter hegemony. In fact, their inclination appears to be premeditated from the manner in which they expand the periodisation employed by Foucault to differentiate the current phase from the 'previous' phase, which includes not only early capitalism but also earlier periods.

> 'Foucault generally refers to the ancien regime and the classical age of French society to illustrate the emergence of disciplinarity, but more generally we could say that the entire first phase of capitalist accumulation (in Europe and elsewhere) were conducted under this paradigm of power. We should understand the society of control, in contrast, as that society (which develops at the far edge of modernity and opens towards the postmodern) in which mechanisms of control become ever more "democratic", ever more immanent to the social field, distributed through the brains and bodies of the citizens.' (H&N, 2000: 41)

This mode of analysis is most confusing. The post-modern notion of over-determination undoubtedly contributes a lot to the Leftist understanding of society – resurrecting it from the straightjackets within which it was for long confined. But that does not mean that we have to eschew analysis. One has to have a specific point of entry into the analytical field. The particular point of entry that we have chosen is dictated by our valorisation of political economy. We have chosen a class entry point and we define classes in terms of their involvement with the processes of production, appropriation and distribution of surplus. We categorically reject the conflation of the notion of the working class to just a dominated segment, which is what the two authors propose.[2] Poetic language, without adequate grounding in a theoretical structure, tends to reduce propositions to simple assertions and frequently lead to internal inconsistencies, as happens in this case also. We will have reason to comment on these inconsistencies soon.

H&N claim a certain lineage for the Empire of global capital. They document 'three exemplary expressions of the utopianism' that serve as the seed from which the thought of counter globalisation, which they propose as the proper course of liberation struggles, grows. These are to be found in the thoughts of Bartolemeȼ de La Casas, Toussaint L'Ouverture, and Karl Marx. Bartolemeȼ was a Christian missionary who witnessed the barbarities of the conquistadors during the enslavement and genocide of the Amerindians, and Toussaint was a slave 'who led the first successful war against modern slavery in the French colony of ... (Haiti)'. The common theme that H&N resurrect from their exhortations is the need to contest the imperialists from within the domain of empire. At this point, the message of *Empire*[3] becomes almost self-critical in its nuances. While their pioneering ideas are hailed, the inherent tendency of these revolutionaries to eulogise the attempts of the enslavers to bring the enslaved under an umbrella of homogeneity – of Christianity, citizens' rights or modernity – is criticised in each particular case, separately. It needs to be noted that these critiques are particular or contingent. H&N do not see these failures as inevitable and accountable by the very nature of the project of 'counter globalisation' proposed by them. The authors see the failure of each of the projects to appreciate the need for diversity as contingent on the particular circumstances in which that project of counter globalisation was conceived. As we see it, these projects are inevitably post-colonial in the sense that has been proposed by Chaudhury et al. (2000). The post-colonial project, as the three authors of *margin of margin* (or *mom* for short) see it, is different from the colonial project. Its discourse is not built on difference between the coloniser and the colonised, while the colonial discourse is openly rooted in the difference and hierarchy of the enslaver and the enslaved culturally and judicially codified by the imperialist. Rather, the discourse of post-colonialism builds on sameness that puts an erasure on difference. In this sense, post-modernism is also an accomplice of this post-colonial project. Post-modernism pretends that everything can and should be seen on an equal plane – constituted by difference and negativity alone. Definition in negativity is one way in which one may exemplify the process of overdetermination. What this conceals, as we have shown in the context of the non-capitalist producer who interacts with the capitalist economic, is that over-determination is always mimicry of overdetermination. That is, the discourse of post-coloniality includes the postcolonised only by denigrating it to the position where it is represented as a position within the (post) imperial culture or discourse but it actually is only a metonym, or a reduced form, of that position. The example that we have discussed in the book is that of the petty producer who can find a place within the analytic description of the capitalist economy only as a worker. But it is actually the position of a reduced form of worker, which the petty producer occupies. Within our theoretic scheme, the projects that H&N hail are post-colonial in nature: you propose counter-globalisation as the proper counter strategy at this moment. You do not see that without a struggle to construct an identity that challenges globalisation, your struggle for an alternative globalisation will always be appropriated within the project of globalisation of capital as some reduced or metonymic position. You will be struggling not to overthrow the hegemony of global capital but to help its mutation to a more acceptable contemporary image. So, what the authors present as aberration, is actually the inherent character of these projects.

The proposal that the 'working class' (or rather, to use H&N's intentionally vague terminology – the 'multitudes') should demand global citizenship is based on the same sort of paternalism that infects the post-colonial projects that H&N discuss. As we have argued throughout the book, the claim that global capital builds a self-sufficient, logical order is a myth. It is necessarily sustained by violence as much as the project of the conquistadors in America or that of the British in India was. To that extent, the project of creating an inclusive discourse within which the wretched of the earth can demand their daily bread and also their liberty is but a post-colonial project. If one were to paint with a broad brush, one would say that while the discourse of the conquistadors and the British and French colonisers belongs to the genre of colonial discourse, the discourse of Bartoleme, Toussaint, Marx on India and H&N belongs to the genre of post-colonial discourse.

A fallout of such discursive accommodation of abolition of slavery, for example, is that it is presented in a purely one-sided way as the victory of the abolitionist movement and defeat of capital. Slave production is initially marked as antithetical to capitalist production, 'since capitalism is based ideologically and materially on free labour, or really on the worker's ownership of his or her labour, capitalism must be antithetical to slave labour'. But soon they go on to argue that the relation is 'more complex'. It is even suggested that the relation may not even be a transitional phenomenon. 'There is no contradiction here: slave labour in the colonies made capitalism in Europe possible, and European capital had no interest in giving it up'. The discursive objective of thus removing the demand for generalised bourgeois freedoms and liberties from the necessary political agenda of the capitalist is to resituate them as aleatory outcomes of a process of conflict. While I agree that attainment of the so-called bourgeois rights is not an inevitable, logically determined objective of capitalist expansion, the problem is that H&N do not argue this on a logical or theoretical plane. Hence the existence and intensity of tension and conflict between the global working-class demand for 'citizens' rights' and the willingness of global capital to fall in line cannot be assigned any theoretical status. So it is possible to think within this under-theorised framework that the demand for universal global citizenship can hit the chain of global capital's domination at its weakest link, as suggested by H&N. A fundamental aspect of the process of abolition of slavery that is overlooked as a result of this weak theorising is that while it is true that abolition is not a necessary aspect of every stage of capitalist expansion, it is also true that it will be a possible outcome of struggle within the overall framework of capitalist domination, only if contemporary capitalism can retain its domination in spite of abolition. This oversight, which is caused by the absence of a theoretical concept that can bring the issue to light, reminds one of the critique of Ranajit Guha's account of colonialism worked out in *mom*. Guha presents certain events during the colonial era in India that show a 'compromise' between the traditional values of Indian culture and the modern values of the imperial culture as instances of partial failure of hegemony of the empire. Chaudhury et al. argue that these do not reveal failure of hegemony but actually reveal the stability of synthetic hegemony. As we have already elaborated, this means that the ruler does not dominate the ruled simply by imposing his/her code on the subjugated. The rules that are imposed are the result of the synthesis of the displaced principles of collaboration of the ruled with the principles of persuasion of the ruler. In any case, the principles of persuasion do not operate in a vacuum. They work on the minds of the subjugated, which thinks within the cultural parameters that are set by his/her existing culture. So, without a synthesis the messages of the ruler would not be decipherable. In the rather one-sided representation of N&H, just as the abolition of slavery is viewed purely as the victory of the abolitionists, it is proposed that the demand for extension of bourgeois freedoms and equalities to the 'multitudes' is a revolutionary demand, the attainment of which will spell defeat for global capital. The question that cannot even begin to be posed is how to determine whether a particular expansion of bourgeois rights and freedoms to geographical and social segments previously excluded is a victory for the ever ongoing struggle to extend such rights or these merely constitute a new component of synthetic hegemony.

Theoretically, the most serious lapse of H&N is the absence of any notion of hegemony (though they use the word quite frequently) and its place in the coercion/persuasion complex that is necessary for maintaining the stability of any power structure. The Gramscian idea of hegemony and its further sophistications inform us that it is possible to mistake the mutation of a ruling order for a defeat of the order. The authors see only the aspect of aspiration for freedom as the basis of abolition, for example. They do not see that abolition of slavery became a reality only when evolution of technology and organisational principles made it profitable to employ 'free' men.

> 'In fact neither moral arguments at home nor calculations of profitability abroad could move European capital to dismantle the slave regimes. *Only* the revolt and the revolution of the slaves themselves could provide an adequate lever. Just as capital moves forward to restructure production and employ new technology *only* as a response to the organised threat of worker antagonism, so too European capital could not relinquish slave production until the organised slaves posed a threat to their power and made that system of production untenable.' (H&N, 2000: 141; italics added)

We will leave the critique at this point because any further journey would take us into the terrain of subjectivity and its role in history. I will leave with the parting observation that while the idea that the master is the subject of history is untenable, the idea that the servant is the subject of history is equally untenable. It is faith in the latter that sustains the belief of H&N that any movement to a greater generality constitutes a victory for the servant. This is the ultimate source of the claim that the demand for more intensive globalisation – the demand for global citizenship by the 'multitudes' – is the proper form of movement that has to be embraced today.

> 'Although Empire has played a role in putting an end to colonialism and imperialism, it nonetheless constructs its own relationship of power based on exploitation that are in many respects more brutal than those it destroyed. The end of the dialectic of modernity has not resulted in the end of the dialectic exploitation. Today nearly all of humanity is absorbed within or subordinated to the network of capitalist exploitation...
>
> Despite recognising all this we insist on asserting that the construction of the empire is a step forward in order to do away with any nostalgia for the power structures that preceded it and refuse any political strategy that involves returning to that old arrangement, such as trying to resurrect the nation-state to protect against global capital.
>
> We claim that Empire is better in the same way that Marx insists that capitalism is better than the forms of society and the modes of production that came before it. Marx's view is grounded in a

> healthy and lucid disgust for the parochial and rigid societies that preceded capitalist society as well as on a recognition that the potential for liberation is increased in the new situation. In the same way we can see that Empire does away with the cruel regimes of modern power and increases the potential for liberation.' (H&N, 2000: 61)

But what is the identity of the 'multitudes' that are to demand global citizenship? Because of the lack of theoretical grounding of the propositions, these 'multitudes' are not fleshed out theoretically. But the problem of situating them within the hegemonic space of global capital is perceived intuitively. That is why H&N ultimately identify the 'multitudes' through their local community that refuses integration into the market nexus!

> 'When the multitude works it produces autonomously and reproduces the entire world of life. Producing and reproducing autonomously *mean producing a new ontological reality*. In effect, *by producing, the multitude produces itself as singularity. It is a singularity that establishes a new place in the non-place of Empire, a singularity that is a reality produced by cooperation, represented by the linguistic community, and developed by the movements of hybridisation. The multitude affirms its singularity by inverting the ideological inversion that all humans on the global surface of the world market are interchangeable*. Standing the ideology of the market on its feet, the multitude promotes through its labour the biopolitical singularizations of groups and sets of humanity, across each and every node of global interchange.' (H&N, 2000: 413, italics added)

We have no quarrels. We have already proposed that the alternative globalisation has to be based on the networking of the local movements that invent the identity of the working people on the basis of the programme of *struggle and construct*. The problem of lack of theoretical ground of the arguments of Hardt and Negri becomes prominent at this point. The diatribe against local movements with which the two set out on their journey, seems to have been abandoned here. They are proposing here, in a rather vague and confusing poetic vein, the constitution of the identity of the working multitudes through their particular heterogeneous work, which refuses homogenisation through the marketplace. So the entire journey comes apparently to nought. The only way, in which one can make sense of the rejection of the agenda of the leftists based on local projects, is by identifying the valuation of these local projects with the demand for power to the nation-state. There is no logical reason for proposing this identity. H&N almost blunder along the blind alley of counter globalisation to the opening provided by *'a reality produced by cooperation, represented by the linguistic community, and developed by the movements of hybridisation. The multitude affirms its singularity by inverting the ideological inversion that all humans on the global surface of the world market are interchangeable'*. We have, on the other hand argued the significance of this identity of the working people through the analysis of exploitation in the era of globalisation.

An important lesson that we can learn from the confusing signals that emanate from a close reading of H&N is that one needs to develop analytical categories to understand the social structures. This of course was most vividly argued by Marx ages ago. What appears as the *immediate* visible reality is simply 'a chaotic conception of the whole' (Marx, 1973). To comprehend the whole in thought it is necessary to first construct analytically simpler categories, that is by the method of abstraction to move to 'simpler conceptions' and thus to the 'simplest determinants'. Having arrived here, 'the journey would have to be retraced' to construct the whole as the result of the 'many determinations and relations' of the simple categories. The point of entry into the second journey is what has been called the *entry point*. The whole that is produced in thought as the result of the many 'determinations and relations' is the over-determined totality. The Rethinking Marxism (RM) School[4] relates this project of construction of the over-determined totality to post-modern insights. This over-determined totality has no essence. All parts determine all others and gain their affectivity through the structured totality. Marxist theory, according to the RM school, is a particular approach to the construction of the overdetermined social totality that uses the working-class position entry point. In the context of the capitalist economic, this entry point means taking the position that commodities are valued according to their abstract labour content. But the working class cannot exist without the capitalist class position.

So we have two ways of valuation of commodities according to the two class positions. The capitalist class position values commodities so as to ensure equal rates of profit and the working class position values commodities according to the abstract labour content. The former are the production prices of commodities and the latter the 'values' (according to the specific use of the word within the field of Marxist political economy). Over-determination, in the context of this economic space, implies that values determine prices and the other way round.

At this point Chaudhury et al. (2000) differ. They show that the system hides a hierarchical relation, which they capture through the conceptual field of 'mimicry of overdetermination'. They say that the 'element that closes an overdetermined field (be that an entry-point concept or a hegemonic nodal point) does not remain neutral to the rest of the system. It privileges a few signifiers or sites and plays down some.' (Chaudhury et al., 2000: 91) They go on to argue that household labour and all labour outside the capitalist sector are denigrated in the course of construction of the order of value and price. Within the scheme of the RM school, the economic relation of the capitalist economic with its outside is viewed as a commodity exchange, which does not involve a 'class process'. By class process is meant a process or a relation through which, over time, there is a flow of surplus value from one class position to another[5], the two class positions being articulated (in an organic sense) through this 'class process'. The relation between a capitalist enterprise and a petty producer is represented as a (non class) commodity exchange because there is an exchange of equivalents or commodities that contain equal values.[6] Chaudhury et al. have shown that such labour can be represented within Marx's theoretical space marked by equal exchange (i.e. in a theoretical space where all commodities sell at the prices of production that are derived from abstract labour values on the basis of the assumption of equality of rates of profit) only on condition that no surplus is retained at the non-capitalist site. They have shown this in the context of household labour, which has been used as a stand-in for the entire set of labour performed outside the capitalist class process and which are a part of the conditions necessary for the reproduction of the capitalist class process. This amounts to reducing household labour and all such to the status of the metonym of the working class. The position of such agents is defined such that they are condemned to produce surplus value for others and so theoretically it is a working class position; but they do not enjoy the privileges of the recognised working class, like legally restricted working hours. So they occupy a position that is a working class position but only in a reduced form. In this sense their positions are referred to as metonyms of the working class position.

In our analysis, the moment of mimicry occurs at the moment of rent appropriation. Rent is sanctioned on the basis of a particular kind of discriminatory right that is obtained not on the basis of some sort of equal exchange in the market but on the basis of extra-market exclusion. We will presently elaborate on the significance of this divergence. But let us first elaborate the further elements of the social structure as conceived in Chaudhury et al. (2000). In order to explain our position, it is essential that we understand the position from which we take off. So let us see the moments of *hegemony.*

To begin with, one has to understand the nuances worked out of the concept of hegemony by Chaudhury (Chaudhury, A., 1988, Chaudhury A., et al., 2000). *Simple hegemony* is attained when the dominant segments of society can persuade the dominated segments (at the level of economic intercourse 'domination' is coterminous with extraction of surplus by the exploiting class[7]) without having to adapt their culture to the cultural ethos of the dominated in any way. The collaboration of the dominated is obtained simply by projecting the persuasive principles of the dominant culture. Such is the hegemony of capital over labour. This is the only kind of hegemony that fits into the scheme of Hegelian dialectics. A stable social system, according to this way of reasoning, is the synthesis of the position of the oppressor and that of the oppressed. In this synthesis the positions of the oppressor/exploiter and that of the oppressed/surplus producer are sublimated into the synthetic totality of which they then appear as logical parts or 'particulars'. When this synthetic order has been spawned, the two positions derive their meaning and significance only from this totality. In contrast, synthetic hegemony is attained when the rulers obtain the consent of the ruled by amalgamation of the modified principles of collaboration of the ruled with the persuasive principles of the ruler. Such occurs, for example in the process of consent that is obtained through the welfarist policies of the World Bank.

Let us pursue the distinction between simple and synthetic hegemony in somewhat greater detail. This discussion is an extension of the discussion in the second section of Chapter 7 on the difference between a culture that can accommodate heterogeneity of entities and a culture that can only cognise homogeneous entities, i.e. entities with differences that are quantifiable – not qualitative differences (in technical terms the heterogeneous is referred to as the concrete, and the homogeneous as the abstract). The working class is defined as a class that has lost ownership of all the means of production other than the power to labour (which cannot be separated from the labourer without denying life). The only way in which the labourer can obtain the wherewithal to survive is to exchange labour power against wages. For this exchange to be possible, it is necessary that the economic space be based on the principle of homogenisation of means of production and products. The labourer cannot survive by consuming the labourer's only possession – the capacity to labour. This therefore has to be quantitatively comparable with the means of life – the commodities that the labourer has to obtain to live. That is, a certain quantity of work performed has to be considered equivalent to a certain quantity of any specific good that the labourer may need for subsistence. Thus the possibility of homogenisation is a necessary condition for the survival of the working class. Everything (embracing every intangible input and produced output) has to have a price tag and so be comparable with everything else. On the other hand, the principle of capital allocation is also based on the possibility of homogenisation. The surplus (value) is to be so distributed among the various parts of capital such that there is equalisation of the rate of profit in all lines of production. This is possible only on condition that all the component parts of real or commodity capital are comparable with each other. For the working class to exist as such, it must submit to the rules of commodity valuation. It must submit to the principle of homogenisation that is essential to valuation. And capital can extract surplus value as profit using these principles. Thus the elementary aspects of the working class culture make it susceptible to collaboration with capital. This is the source of 'economism' that has always plagued leftist practice in capitalist countries. This is simple hegemony of capital over labour.

The culture of the forest dwellers, who refuse to accede to commodity exchange, is anathema to this elementary aspect of bourgeois culture. They resist the attempt to reduce their native culture or way of life to a monetary equivalent. But once they are reduced to the refugees of development, crowding the fringes of the urban spaces, their old tribal values are transformed or 'displaced' into a different kind of community culture that can negotiate with the commodity culture of capital. They inhabit not the so-called civil society of the urban citizens but a sub-city where rule by the organic leaders of the community is replaced by various displacements of such leadership into extra-constitutional authorities that dispense both justice and benevolence. Such authority (which goes by various names in Bengal, like *'para committee'* and *'colony committee'*) is also a source of authoritarian power for the existing dispensation at the formal level, as also of a potent means of vote mobilisation. (Again, these may also serve as a focus for mobilisation against the global order or the existing dispensation.) Their demands can be negotiated within the capitalist order unlike the non-negotiable demands that were raised from their original community space. As forest dwellers they demanded, for example, that they should not be displaced under any circumstance because the forest was the source of their unique way of life, which could not be compared to any other and so could not be monetarily evaluated. As refugee communities, they now demand monetary compensation for the loss of their way of life. They demand that urban legality should be relaxed to condone their settler colonies on the fringes of urban society. The emergent culture of the new community is accommodated by the culture of capital and so emerges the 'human face of capital' that is reflected in the 'welfarist principles' of, say, the World Bank. The displaced people's community principles are distorted to obtain the principles of collaboration of the refugees – the demands that this community now makes are the principles of collaboration. These are based on the culture of homogenisation through the market.[8]

Another important aspect where our ideas can be elaborated upon within the theoretic space elaborated by *mom* (the acronym of Chaudhury A., et al. 2000 – *margin of margin*) is the aspect of post-colonialism. To the authors of *mom*, post-colonialism is colonialism without a subject (Chaudhury A., et al., 2000, p.176). While in the colonial space denigration of the colonised is willed by the colonising power, denigration of the post-colonised within the space of the post-colony is structurally inevitable: it is independent of the subjective will of the post-coloniser. Non-capital is the post-colony of capital. It must denigrate it to represent it within the economic discursive site. This formulation is particularly helpful in constructing the theoretical space of globalisation. Globalisation is the era when imperialism is decentred, as we have discussed. So the subject, the imperialist, is absent as a theoretical entity. Its presence and so its location is contingently determined by a fact that is beyond the discursive space of *mom*: the interweaving of PCA with the capitalist process. To put it pithily, *mom does not leave a space for violence as necessary and coterminous with global capital. The need for the imperial state(s) arises because of the presence of violence within the order of capital. This violence, perpetrated by PCA, is outside the pale of the theoretic space marked out by mom. And this is where we part ways with mom and also with Marx of Capital.*

As a corollary of our revaluation of the place of violence in the order of global capital, we have rejected the division of class processes (i.e. social processes through which surplus of social output is produced, appropriated, distributed and spent) into 'fundamental' and 'subsumed'. This is a division that is there in *Capital* and, which has been used to telling effect by the RM group. A fundamental class process is one through which surplus is produce and appropriated. A subsumed class process is a process through which surplus is distributed, received. (We have touched upon this in footnote 102.) This division is used to show that, among other differences, the difference between the process of rent 'receipt' and the process of profit 'appropriation' can be captured in terms of the division into fundamental and subsumed class processes. While the process of profit appropriation is a fundamental capitalist class process, the process of rent receipt is a subsumed class process. It is argued that surplus value production and appropriation occurs at the site of the economic process that relates the capitalist and the worker. At this site, surplus value is produced and appropriated by capital. Subsequently, capital distributes portions of the appropriated surplus value to other class and non-class positions. These secondary payments are made in order to ensure that the conditions of capitalist class process are reproduced within the social order. For example, tax payment is such a subsumed class payment. It is made in order that the state should be enabled to perform the economic and non-economic activities that are necessary to sustain the capitalist class process. Rent payment is a subsumed class payment that is made in order that land and other natural resources should be made available for continued capitalist production.

The separation of rent and profit as belonging to different categories of class payments effectively erases the possibility of sighting/situating the violence that closes the gaps in the so-called rational order of the capitalist system. We do not accept this closure and so, this erasure. It can be shown that once rent is introduced into the system, the observable division of the value of social produce between necessary and surplus value, is affected. We have seen how rent changes relative prices. This would change the value of output that is deemed to be necessary for the reproduction of productive labour. Naturally, this would also change the value of the fraction that constitutes surplus value. But this claim is rooted in the presumption that value calculations are based on the prices that are determined in a theoretical field where we allow the existence of rent. Within the field of unreconstituted Marxian theory (for example, *Capital*, RM and Chaudhury et al., Chaudhury and Ray Chaudhury) value calculations are not affected by the presence/absence and magnitude of rent payment. Value and its division into necessary and surplus are calculated on the basis of prices but not the observed market prices, which would be disturbed by rent, among other things. The prices that are employed in the calculation of value within the scheme of RM are the prices that would equate the rates of profit across sectors, assuming the existence of only fundamental class payments – profit and wages. Thus both systems can be argued to be logical in their own way. Two fundamentally different systems cannot be evaluated logically. One entry point is not superior to another; it is so thoroughly different (i.e. situated on a totally different plane of representation) that there is no comparability.

If you denigrate rent payment to the status of a subsumed class payment, there is no way that you can claim that violence is fundamental to the capitalist system. This denigration inevitably brings in its train corollaries that we have talked of. For one thing, the process of PCA has to be reduced to the chronologically prior stage. That is, the word 'primitive' has to be interpreted in the chronological sense. Our position, in contrast, is that in the current age of globalisation, the violent distortion of rights in order to extract rent is the fundamental character of capital. Thus the assignment of PCA to the realm of the chronologically primitive, robs us of the possibility of understanding the basic tendency of capital in this age.

It is beyond the scope of this enquiry to try to understand why Marx and Marxism had/has this tendency to construct a theoretical space where the capitalist economic can only be explicated as a logical and self-sufficient entity. But there does appear to have been a certain Eurocentrism in Marx and most of Marxist theory. This is perhaps the reason for attributing the backwardness of the Orient to the existence of a specific mode of production outside the succession of evolving stages that constitute the history of Europe – the Asiatic mode of production. We are not saying that this indicates any jingoism. This was probably the effect of the modernising philosophy in which European thought was enmeshed. Particularly the impact of Hegel was perhaps more than the post-modern readings of Marx suggest. This position implies that there is at least a structural or discursive jingoism in Marxism.

This tendency to construct a difference between the two sides of the imperial divide was common to the imperial historians and to modernisers like Marx. Therefore, there was an expectation that the opening up of the underdeveloped world to interaction with the West would be positively beneficial to the East as it would lead to the growth of capitalism or to modernity, according to the subjective proclivity of the particular theory.

The vision of Marx[9] and classical Marxists in general has not been realised. Capitalism has failed to displace non-capitalist formations in economies with which it has come into contact, through violent colonisation or otherwise. All these theories diagnosed the cause of underdevelopment of the poor countries to be situated within these countries. They had all prophesied that the spread of various levels of exchange between the underdeveloped and the developed nations would *modernise* the *backward*, poor countries. But the fact was that such exchange was only worsening the condition in the poor countries. This was theorised by the Dependency School (DS) fathered by Frank (Frank, A.G., 1978) as well as by the World System (WS) approach of Wallerstein (Wallerstein, I., 1979). These schools emerged out of the empirical work of the United Nations Economic Commission for Latin America (ECLA). ECLA argued that from the middle of the nineteenth to the late twentieth century, the development of Latin America was oriented towards increasing commerce with the capitalist world. Empirically, it was observed that this was also the period of increasing immiserisation. From this they argued that trade did not lead to the accrual of benefits all round but to prosperity for some and misery for most. This was later theorised by the DS into the proposition that development was not a worldwide phenomenon, but that development in *the centre* caused underdevelopment in *the periphery.* The entire world was linked through an unbroken chain, each of whose links was made up of a relation between a *metropolis* and a *satellite.* The metropolis extracted surplus from the satellite and this was both the source of the metropolis' prosperity as well as the cause of the backwardness of the satellite.

The DS argued that the entire system was ordered by the systemic needs of the centre or metropolis. Thus the difference between the centre and the periphery or satellite could be captured in terms of the articulation/disarticulation binary. The parts of the economy of the centre were integrated or articulated with one another directly. Very roughly, one can think of this as some sort of a balance among the various sectors of the economy. On the other hand, the different sectors of the economy of the periphery are disarticulated. They are articulated into a system only via the centre. For example, a part of the peripheral economy may be manufacturing parts for highly sophisticated machinery. This sector has no production linkage with the rest of the peripheral economy. Viewed from the perspective of the peripheral economy alone, this sector would not be economically viable. It is only when we think of this as related to the centre that the reason for its existence becomes evident. The machinery is sold to the centre to obtain funds, for example, with which that part of the peripheral economy can purchase the wherewithal to survive from the manufacturer of these commodities in the underdeveloped periphery. This articulation/disarticulation gives to the centre the power to control the markets through which this interlocking is achieved. Control, in turn, allows the metropolis to suck out the surplus from the satellite. The WS is not substantially different from the DS perspective. Its focus is somewhat different. It tries to explain why the world capitalist system centres on accumulation at the centre of the system, while the older imperial world orders thrived on extravagant expenditure by the centre. This periodisation led to a debate between DS and WS regarding the base period when capitalism could be said to have developed as a world system. This is not relevant to our discussion.

These theories marked a great divide in Marxist theoretical space. It had been customary to attribute the 'backwardness' of the colonies and the post-colonies to their internal structure. The enunciation of the Asiatic Mode is one such example. The DS and WS approaches broke these European shackles and pointed fingers at the developed capitalist world. I agree wholeheartedly with this position. They were the first to point out that development and underdevelopment complemented each other. Seen purely in terms of effects, our position is similar: we have maintained that the survival and continuous expansion of capitalism demands continuous PCA and PCA produces the refugees of development – the wretched of globalisation. They are accommodated in the non-capitalist economy that is not independent of global capital. Capital extracts surplus even from this sector through various forms of rent.

Our fundamental difference from these theories is that while both the DS and the WS theories explain the link between the developed and underdeveloped parts in terms of conjuncture or history, we explain it through the theoretic space of the capitalist economy. By reviving PCA from the past and integrating it into the present of the capitalist of economy and, as a corollary, removing the distinction between fundamental and subsumed class processes, we have established development and underdevelopment as intertwined processes within the very theoretical space of capital. This difference is particularly significant in the present context, when capital has become global. Within the scheme of DS and WS, the metropolis and periphery have definite geographical locations. Once the link between development and underdevelopment is raised from its conjunctural location and inserted into the theoretical space of capital, geographical location of the parts becomes indefinite and conjunctural. Global capital does not need to be geographically centred at a particular location.

There is another kind of explanation of the phenomenon of survival and even expansion of the marginalised or so-called informal sector that has been championed by a section of the left in India. In recent times, Sanyal (2007) has argued this position most coherently. Very briefly, the position is that transfer of surplus from the 'formal' capitalist sector sustains the 'informal sector' in order to manufacture consent of the masses to rule by capital. Gramsci's idea that the ruling combination of classes or class segments maintain their control over the subordinated classes or class segments both through coercion and persuasion is at the heart of this stand. The need for persuasion, presumably, is greater in a country with a formal democratic system of governance than in a country where an autocratic regime is in power. Persuasion is, therefore, all the more necessary in India than, say, in Pakistan under military rule. As it spreads, global capital dispossesses large segments of the workforce. The dispossessed or the refugees of development and the workers who have lost their jobs cannot be employed in capitalist production, in spite of its expanding size. The capital-intensive nature of growth precludes their absorption in the labour force working in capitalist enterprise. This is termed as 'surplus population', to distance this segment from Marx's 'reserve army of unemployed'. They are in excess of the segment required to constitute a reserve army. This surplus population poses a political threat to the ruling combination within a democratic polity because of their significant numbers. To pacify this vast mass, they have to be accommodated in the informal sector, run generally on non-capitalist lines, though there may be small capitalist concerns also. The sector is variously named as 'need economy', 'subsistence economy' or 'informal sector'. It cannot generate sufficient value to ensure its own reproduction. So, in order to buy consent of the excess population, capital transfers resources to this sector, via the state, to ensure the conditions of reproduction of this sector.[10] Such resource transfer takes place in many ways, which are informal or not legally recordable. For example, they may be allowed to hawk their wares on pavements. This is a thoroughly illegal provision of public thoroughfare for private business. This is an informal transfer that the state virtually legalises. The state provides the necessary civic infrastructure without realising any taxes from them. Their 'illegal' dwellings in shanties huddled just adjacent to railway tracks (on railway property) are tolerated by the state. This is at the cost, in terms of time of the formal sector inhabitants. The resources provided by the state to the informal sector are funded by the transfer of resources from the capitalist sector to the state through various forms of taxes. The claim that the informal sector is protected and fostered in the poor countries like India is buttressed by the notion of governmentality. This means, according to the definition provided by Sanyal (2007), that 'interventions on the part of the developmental state (and non-state organizations) to promote the well-being of the population (and what can be identified as a *reversal of primitive accumulation*) refers to this realm of welfarist governmentality: the creation of the need-economy is an imperative of governance'. The introduction of the notion of governmentality reduces the significance of the distinction between formal democracies and autocratic regimes, according to Sanyal. Governmentality is an ideological requirement that must be fulfilled by all states today, as I understand Sanyal's position.

This contribution is important because it is a serious attempt to understand a vast sector of the economy that is left out of the capitalist economic within the Marxist discourse. It is important for the purpose we set out at the beginning of the chapter because Sanyal deals with an economic space that is significant to our position – the informal sector.[11] Also, Sanyal professes to a Marxist epistemology. It is doubly interesting to me because Sanyal claims just the opposite of what is a central thesis of our present endeavour. He claims that there is a reverse PCA towards the informal sector, while we have laboured to show a PCA from the outside of the space of global capitalist enterprise. My great discomfort with this exposition is that this is an attempt to totally ignore the economic intercourse between the formal and the informal sectors and reconstitutes the developed-underdeveloped unity within the space of polity. Within Sanyal's scheme, the articulation of the capitalist and non-capitalist or informal sectors is achieved at the level of polity alone. The definition of the parts is however at the level of the economic. This rules out mutual constitutivity of the two sectors. This goes against the very grain of the epistemological position to which Sanyal lays claim – over-determination. The need economy and the accumulation economy are defined autonomously. The concept of need becomes unhinged from any social mooring. It can be defined, measured and treated only by governmentality.

I have no quarrels with Catholicism in choice of theory to 'explain' an 'event' in history. We all frequently resort to it. After all, explanations are mostly meant to persuade. My objection is that this adherence to modernism ultimately works in the service of global capital. The denial of any theoretical space for thinking mutual constitutivity shuts out both the possibility of conflict and collaboration between the informal sector (or need sector) and the modern sector (or the accumulation sector). This theoretical compartmentalisation also rules out the ability of the theoretical space to take account of the economic intercourse between the two sectors. Thus the possibility of surplus being channelled off from the informal sector to the modern sector is shut out, and this is what has been the key to our understanding of the relation between the capitalist sector and the non-capitalist sector in our scheme. Just as the principle of unity constructed at the level of polity, in Sanyal's scheme, is built on the premise of 'reverse PCA', it could have been constructed on the premise of PCA.[12] The point that we are making is that there is no theoretical space for accommodating structural-economic causality. This blindness also denigrates the struggle of the informal sector workers to secure their 'community rights'. It appears in Sanyal's scheme that whatever they have got (the informal right to hawk their goods on the pavements, the illegal right (!) to live on railway land in makeshift shanties, etc.) is largesse bestowed on them by capital to satisfy the principle of governmentality. In our scheme, these concessions are wrung out[13] of the government through a struggle, in the course of which the refugees of development define their new communities.

In our conception of the economy, need is an ethical concern of the community of the working people. It is not defined autonomously and is contingent to their situation in terms of geography, and the history of the community's coming into being. The dwellers on the banks of the Narmada, when faced with the threat of eviction, demanded that their existing life and livelihood should not be disturbed. When the movement could not force the government to go back on its plan, the demand of the community changed to the demand to restrict the height of the dam. With increasing height of dam and displacement of villagers, the demand of the village community changed to proper compensation. When such displaced persons flock to the urban fringes as unrecorded urban inhabitants, they form new communities. Their demands change. Their demand, as the inhabitants of the sub-city, is that they be informally allowed life and livelihood. That is, their 'illegal' shanties and occupations should not be subjected to 'legal' and police harassment. They organise to pressure the government to fulfill their demand at every stage. The extent to which their demands are conceded by the government depends on the outcome of pressures and counter pressures. It is not the result of any largesse on the part of the formal sector. Their demands are largely in conflict with bourgeois legal propriety. But when the state threatens – under pressure from the capitalist or formal sector – to impose various forms of bourgeois propriety like eviction (!) the settlers counter-strategy involves mostly the demand that they be conferred bourgeois rights either to the lands they have occupied or on alternative lands of their choice. Our analysis suggests that capital, or the formal sector if you like, is willing to negotiate with the marginalised because the refugees of development will ultimately produce surplus for it. 'Governmentality' is too under-theorised a concept to be amenable to critical evaluation. But neither is there much insight offered by this concept. When any economic event is not explainable by the logic of the economic, it can be explained by some stretch of 'governmentality'.

Let us end this conversation on a self-critical note. The construction of the local as counter-hegemonic strategy in the age of hegemony of global capital has to continuously criticise itself from within. One has to be ever watchful against the possibility of subversion of the project by fundamentalism or sectarianism of leftist or rightist persuasion.[14] This has been the bane of many people's movements in our country that have petered out or have been isolated and repressed by the state.

The constructed community of the local, which is to be the bulwark of the struggle against the global, has the terrible potential of regressing to communalism.

NOTES

1. Marx calls this the "chaotic conception of the whole". (Marx, Karl, 1973:100)
2. There is an interesting and highly thought provoking, though rather obtuse, discussion on the difference between a position based on categorisation of the population on the basis of some cultural (or sometimes just inarticulate) notion like domination and categorisation on the basis of the notion of classes (i.e. economic exploitation) (Spivak, G. 1985)
3. The book is referred to in italics.
4. See note 1 of Chapter 1.
5. They, very consciously, use the term 'class position' rather than the term 'class' because they want to signify that a person who works in a factory, for example, is not just a worker but is also father, a husband, maybe a religious fundamentalist and so on. In different situations the same person occupies different positions. Within the work relation or the class process the person occupies the working class position.
6. There are various subtleties in the RM position to which we cannot do full justice here. For example, they differentiate – following Marx – between fundamental class process and subsumed class process. The former consist of class processes where surplus value is produced and appropriated (the process that relates the working class position and the capitalist class position) and the latter consists of class processes through which surplus is distributed and received (for example that which occurs between the capitalist position, as payer of corporate tax and the government as the receiver of such payment). From this pair of definitions it follows that any process that does not involve a flow of surplus value between the two positions between whom the process occurs is not a class process. In this sense the relation between a petty producer (who sells some input to a capitalist enterprise and the capitalist enterprise) and the capitalist enterprise is not a class relation.
7. There is a different or supplementary view of economic domination that occurs in Sanyal (2007) among others. According to this view, there can be a segment of the population that is excluded from the economic in the sense that it is neither a site

of production nor of extraction or receipt of surplus value produced within the capitalist economic site. Yet this marginal segment, that Sanyal refers to as the informal sector, is politically necessary to the maintenance of the capitalist sector because it provides a subsistence cushion to those excluded from the process of capitalist progress for various reasons. So this sector has to be maintained and dominated by capital. So we have economic domination without surplus extraction. We shall presently distance ourselves from such positions and see why this is not economic domination in the way we see things.

8. Let us take a rather grotesque example of this process of homogenisation that may help elaborate the position. In the process of dislodging peasants from their land and community for capital to expand there is frequently rape and pillage. Where the state directly undertakes such operation at the behest of capital the public hue and cry is likely to be more sustained. The state may even be compelled to pay 'compensation'. In such cases the government pays different rates of compensation. One for death! One for rape and one for injury! The judiciary also sanctifies this because the courts sometimes award such compensation. So we have a reduction of life and body to monetary magnitudes.
9. 'The country that is more developed only shows to the less developed, the image of its own future' Marx, Karl, 1954.
10. Though this position has been hailed as offering a fundamental new insight, this is hardly new:

    "The modern laborer, on the contrary, instead of rising with the progress of industry, sinks deeper and deeper below the conditions of existence of his own class. He becomes a pauper, and pauperism develops more rapidly than population and wealth. And here it becomes evident, that the bourgeoisie is unfit any longer to be the ruling class in society, and to impose its conditions of existence upon society as an over-riding law. It is unfit to rule because it is incompetent to assure an existence to its slave within his slavery, because it cannot help letting him sink into such a state, that it has to feed him, instead of being fed by him." *The Communist Manifesto*; Marx, Karl: Sec.1.
11. The nuances in definition are not important as I see it.
12. It should be obvious that our position emphasises the process of PCA. We do not deny that the process of exclusion as a possibility. Sanyal's exposition has highlighted this aspect of capitalist growth. This needs to be mentioned, but at the same time its

obvious weaknesses should be understood if we are to go ahead.

13. 'Wrung out' is an expression, which in this case also accommodates the aspect of negotiation, i.e. mutual concessions. There is negotiation, for example, regarding the pavements on which the hawkers will be allowed to trade their wares. The formal sector employees, who constitute the urban affluent are loath to see 'their pavements being 'usurped', but their elected representatives negotiate. Also, while the position of the urban dweller demands that the hawker be banished from the city, the position of the purchaser of consumer goods – which the same functionary occupies at another time – demands that they be accommodated, because they sell at low prices. There may sometimes be a distinction between the persons who occupy these positions. The husband, who does not shop demands their eviction, the wife wants that they be accommodated. Again the elected representatives are not wholly defined by the fact of representing 'the people of the locality'; they also represent various political parties. They have to accommodate the fringe elements, because by the very nature of their existence they have less regard for formal legality and can, therefore lend muscle power to the party and the elected representative, whenever necessary.
14. One can elucidate this limitation of our proposal by referring back to our sketchy remarks about the new marginal communities formed by the displaced victims of development who flock to the margins of the cities. "They do not inhabit the so-called civil society of the urban citizens but a sub-city where rule by the organic leaders of the community is replaced by various displacements of such leadership into extra-constitutional authorities that dispense both justice and benevolence. Such authority (which goes by various names in Bengal, like *'para committee'* and *'colony committee'*) is also a source of authoritarian power for the existing dispensation as also of a potent means of vote mobilisation." Such communities of marginalised working people hardly show the potential that we are glorifying!

References

AMR, 2006; "Land grab and Development Fraud in India"; editorial in *Analytical Monthly Review*, September 2006, Kharagpur.

Bailey, A.M.and Llobera,J.R., 1981; *The Asiatic Mode of Production*; Bailey, A.M. and Llobera, J.R.. RKP, London, 1981.

Basu, P. and Sanyal, S., 1992; *Sangharsh o Nirman*; (Eds.) Basu, Purnendu and Sanyal, Shankar; Anushtup, Calcutta, 1992.

Basu, P. K., 2001; *Asiatic Feudalism, Capitalism and (non)Transition*; Basu, Pranab Kanti; Ph.D. dissertation; Department of Economics, Calcutta University, Kolkata, 2001.

Basu, P. K., 2007; "Political Economy of Land Grab", Basu, Pranab Kanti; *Economic and Political Weekly*, Mumbai, (42:14).

Baudrillard, J., 1984; "The Precession of Simulacra", Baudrillard, Jean; In Brian Wallis (Ed.): *Art After Modernism: Rethinking Representations*, Vol. 1. New York: Museum of Contemporary Art (reprinted from *Art and Text* 11 (September 1983): 3-47.

Bhattacharyya, Sabyasachi, 1999; *The Mahatma and the Poet: Letters and Debates between Gandhi and Tagore 1915-1941; Compiled and Edited by* Sabyasachi Bhattacharyya; National Book Trust, New Delhi, 1997.

Bobbio, R., 1979 "Gramsci and the Conception of Civil Society"; Bobbio, Roberto in *Gramsci & Marxist Theory*; (Eds.) Mouffe, Chantal. RKP, London, 1979.

Chakraborti, A. and Cullenberg, S., 2003; *Transition and Development in India*; Chakraborti, Anjan and Cullenberg, Stephen; Routledge; New Delhi, 2003.

Chandler, D., net. *Semiotics for Beginners*; Daniel Chandler @www.aber.ac.uk/media/Documents/S4B/semiotic.html

Chatterjee, P., 1986; *Nationalist Thought and the Colonial Discourse*; Chatterjee, Partha; Oxford University Press, Delhi, 1986.

Chatterjee, P., 1994; *The Nation and its Fragments*; Chatterjee, Partha; Oxford University Press, Delhi, 1994.

Chaudhury, A., 1988; "From Hegemony to Counter Hegemony"; Chaudhury,Ajit; *Economic and Political Weekly: Review of Political Economy*, Bombay, (23:3).

Chaudhury, Ajit, 1992; *Equality beyond Equality*; Chaudhury, Ajit; Anushtup, Calcutta, 1992.

Chaudhury,A. and Ray Chaudhury, S., 2003; "Feudocapitalism"; Chaudhury, Ajit, and Ray Chaudhury, Sarthak; *Other Voice*, Kolkata, 2003.

Chaudhury, A. and Chakraborti, A., 2000; "The Market Economy and the Marxist Economists: Through the lens of a Housewife"; Chaudhury, Ajit and Chakraborti, Anjan; *Rethinking Marxism*, July, 2000.

Chaudhury, A., et. al., 2000; *margin of margin: Profile of an Unrepentant Postcolonial Collaborator*; Chaudhury, Ajit, Das, Dipankar, and Chakraborti, Anjan; Anushtup, Calcutta, 2000.

Chaudhury, A., 2001; "Western Marxists Commodity Fetishism: Looking for an Exit"; *from the margins (Of Development and Beyond)*, (Ed.) Chakrabarti, Anjan, et.al., (I:II), August, 2001, Kolkata.

Dubey, M., 1992; "The Political Economy of the Uruguay Round of Trade Negotiations", Dubey, Muchkund in *Dunkel's Draft Text: Critical Analysis*, (Ed.) National Working Group on Patent Laws, New Delhi, July 1992.

Evans, D., 1966; *An Introductory Dictionary of Lacanian Psychology*; Evans, Dylan; Routledge, New York, 1996.

Foucault, M., 1994; *The Order of Things*; Foucault, Michelle, Vintage Books, 1994, New York.

Frank, A. G., 1978; *Dependent Accumulation and Underdevelopment*; Frank, Andre Gunder; M.R.Press, New York, 1978.

Friedman, M., 1958; "Foreign Economic Aid: Means and Objectives"; Friedman, Milton; *YaleRreview*, vol. 47. Excerpts published in *Foreign Aid*; (Ed.) Bhagwati, J. and Eckaus, R.S.; Penguin Books Ltd., Middlesex, England, 1970.

Fukuyama, F., 1992; *The End of History and The Last Man*; Fukuyama, Francis; Avon, New York, 1992.

Gandhi, M., 1910; *"Hind Swaraj", The Collected Works of Mahatma Gandhi*, Vol. 10; Publications Division, Government of India, New Delhi, 1958 onwards.

Gangully, B.N., 1977; *Indian Economic Thought: Nineteenth Century Perspectives*; Gangully, B.N.; Tata McGraw-Hill Publishing Co., New Delhi, 1977.

Hardt, M. and Negri, A., 2000; *Empire*; Hardt, M. and Negri, A.; Harvard University Press, Harvard, 2000.

Hegel, G.W.F., 1952; *Philosophy of Right*; G.W.F.; Translated by Knox, T.M.; Encyclopaedia Britannica, Great Books, 1952.

Hegel G.W.F., Logic; *Logic* (also known as "*Short Logic*") at Hegel.net; *Encyclopaedia of the Physical Sciences Part One*.

Laclau, E. and Mouffe, C., 2001; *Hegemony and Socialist Strategy: Towards a Radical Democratic Politics*; Ernesto Laclau and Chantal Mouffe; Verso, (2nd Edition) 2001.

Lenin, V.I., 1992; *State and Revolution*; Lenin, V.I.; Translated by Robert Service; Penguin Classics, 1992.

Mao Tse-tung, 1962; "Talk at an Enlarged Central Work Conference, 1962" published in *Mao Tse-Tung Unrehearsed*; Edited by Stuart Schram, Penguin Books, England, 1974.

Marx, K., 1954; *Capital, Vol. I*, Marx, Karl; Progress Publishers, Moscow, 1954; reprint, 1974.

Marx, K., 1959; *Capital, Vol. III*, Marx, Karl; Progress Publishers, Moscow, 1959; reprint, 1974.

Marx, K., 1969; *The Communist Manifesto*, Marx, Karl; Tr. Samuel Moore in cooperation with Frederick Engels, 1888; in *Marx/Engels Selected Works, Volume I*, Progress Publishers, Moscow, USSR, 1969.

Marx, K., 1973; *Grundrisse*; Marx, Karl (translated by Martin Niclaus); Pelican Books, Penguin Books Ltd., London, 1973 (reprint, 1974).

Peet, R., 2003; *Unholy Trinity: the IMF, World Bank and WTO*; Peet, Richard; Zed Books, London and New York, 2003.

Resnick, S.A. and Wolff, A.R., 1987; *Knowledge and Class*; Resnick, S.A. and Wolff, A.R.; The University of Chicago Press, Chicago, 1987.

Ross, S., net.; "A Very Brief Introduction to Lacan"; Ross, Stephen; saross at uvic.ca.net.

Sanyal, K., 2007; *Rethinking Capitalist Development: Primitive Accumulation, Governmentality and the Post-colonial Capitalism*; Sanyal, K.; Routledge, New Delhi, 2007.

Spivak, G., 1985; "Speculations on the Question of Value" Spivak, Gayatri Chakravorty; *Diacritics*, Vol 15, no. 4 (Winter 1985); John Hopkin University Press.

Sturrock, J., 2002; *Structuralism*; Sturrock, John; Blackwell publishing Professionals, London, 2002.

Tagore, R. N., 1905; "*Swadeshi Samaj*" in *Atmashakti, Rabindra Rachanabali, Vol. III*, Collected Works of Rabindranath Tagore; Publications Dept., Visva-Bharati, Kolkata, 1905.

Wallerstein, I., 1979; *The Capitalist World Economy*; Wallerstein, I.; Cambridge University Press, Cambridge, 1979.

Index